W9-AAN-996

A COLLECTION OF FAVORITE QUILTS

NARRATIVES, DIRECTIONS & PATTERNS FOR 15 QUILTS

By Judy Florence

American Quilter's Society
P.O. Box 3290
Paducah, KY 42002-3290

ACKNOWLEDGMENTS

Thanks to...

Pat Simonsen, for sharing the fruits of her quilt frame and computer – "My Stars! A Computer Quilt" and Christmas Ribbons;

Marie Halmstad, for taking such good care of her French Basket;

Paula Jones, for her precision-pieced Arabic Lattice;

Chippewa County Friends, for their generous gift of friendship blocks;

and to

Kathy Bartel, Dorothy Gilbertson, Maggie Gustafson, and *Sue Terman,* for sharing from their quilt collections.

Dedication page photo by the Author.
All other photographs by **Jim Christoffersen**

Additional copies of this book may be ordered from:

American Quilter's Society
P.O. Box 3290
Paducah, KY 42002-3290

@$18.95. Add $1.00 for postage & handling.

Copyright: Judy Florence, 1990

This book or any part thereof may not be reproduced without the written consent of the Author and Publisher.

DEDICATION
To my son, David. This one's for you.

Table of Contents

"A special language exists among quiltmakers.
Their words and thoughts are expressed in patterns, fabrics,
quilting designs, and colors that they use in their quilts.
To know their quilts is to understand them in a very special way."

Mary Golden, author of
The Friendship Quilt Book
(Yankee Publishing)

Introduction

PICKING A FAVORITE

If you were asked "What is your favorite quilt?" colorful designs and alluring patterns would quickly come to mind. If the question were put to a large group of quilters, myriads of lovely quilt images would come into mental focus. Responses to the question would be many and varied, with clusters of votes for time-honored favorites like the Lone Star, Rose of Sharon, and the Log Cabin, with a scattering of choices among lesser known patterns, all chosen for reasons varying from technical to strictly personal.

This book is about a few favorite quilts. It is not about a quilt popularity contest. These fifteen quilts will not be everyone's favorites. No scientific survey on favorite quilts was conducted. I didn't ask anybody else to tell me about their favorite quilts. The only person to whom I mentioned my collection of favorite quilts book project said, "How can you have more than one favorite? I thought you could only have one favorite of anything." I knew full well that I couldn't write a book about a one-and-only favorite quilt. In the world of quilts, most of us know that to narrow the choice to only one favorite would be an arduous if not impossible task.

If the general public were asked about their favorite quilts, the responses would probably center on the familiar; or maybe on colors – beautiful colors – or designs that bring back memories. People like familiar quilt patterns, pretty colors, and impressive quilting stitches. One of the "people's favorites" in my quilt collection is the Rose of Sharon: a well-known "natural" pattern (everybody likes roses), lovely colors (soft pinks and shady greens), and oodles of hand quilting.

"Something regarded with special favor or liking" is how my dictionary defines favorite, not the best, the most beautiful, or the most outstanding, although several of the quilts in this book qualify in these categories, too. When the favorite quilt is contemplated, it usually conjures up an image of something with a personal touch or connection. We wouldn't all agree on the favorite. And I don't think we would want to.

So this is really a book of some of MY favorite quilts, selected for different reasons. Some were chosen with consideration of what friends, students, or judges have indicated they like, by response at an exhibition or in a class, or by the bestowing of an award such as viewer's choice or judge's choice. Others were selected because they possess distinctive characteristics, perhaps something nostalgic or sentimental, perhaps something innovative in design or style.

FIFTEEN FAVORITE QUILTS

As you page through the book, you will discover quilt patterns covering a variety of dates, styles, and techniques. A span of sixty years is covered, beginning with an exquisite 1929 appliqued French Basket and continuing to a 1989 computer-designed Star Quilt. A 1939 Album friendship is included, also a Lone Star pieced with Thirties fabrics.

The quilts are from my personal collection or from the collection of friends in the Eau Claire, Wisconsin vicinity. The maker or owner of each quilt is specified at the beginning of each chapter.

I have included a mixture of both traditional and innovative quilt designs, from the ever popular Sunbonnet Sue to an intriguing Arabic Lattice. There's also a crib quilt, several friendship quilts, old familiar patterns in new settings, scrap quilts, and a quilt made from recycled bags. Hopefully, there's something for everybody.

The quilt patterns have been summarized according to construction method (pieced or appliqued), size (large / bed size or small / lap, crib, or wall), style (traditional or contemporary), and suitability for scrap design.

PIECED	APPLIQUED
Virginia Reel	Sunbonnet Sue
Attic Windows	Rose of Sharon
Lone Star	Computer Star
Four-Patch Album	French Basket
Album	
Improved Nine-Patch	
Ocean Waves	
Favorite Creatures	
Arabic Lattice	
Christmas Ribbons	
Rice Bag Quilt	

If you are looking for a larger commitment, a bed-size project, there are several from which to choose. For a lesser commitment, select from the six smaller projects:

LARGE *(Twin bed / larger)* SMALL *(Lap, crib, wall)*
Lone Star   Virginia Reel
Album   Attic Windows
Improved Nine-Patch   Four-Patch Album
Ocean Waves   Favorite Creatures
Sunbonnet Sue   Arabic Lattice
Rose of Sharon   Christmas Ribbons
Computer Star
French Basket
Rice Bag Quilt

If you prefer a traditional pattern, you have eight patterns from which to choose. The remaining seven designs can be considered contemporary, or at least contemporary interpretations of traditional patterns.

TRADITIONAL   CONTEMPORARY
Lone Star   Virginia Reel
Four-Patch Album   Attic Windows
Album   Computer Stars
Improved Nine-Patch   Favorite Creatures
Ocean Waves   Arabic Lattice
Sunbonnet Sue   Christmas Ribbon
Rose of Sharon   Rice Bag Quilt
French Basket

At least ten of the quilts can be made with scraps or accumulated fabric mixtures, with little additional fabric investment. Try matching these patterns with your scrap bag:

SCRAP QUILTS
Virginia Reel   Attic Windows
Lone Star   Four-Patch Album
Album   Improved Nine-Patch
Ocean Waves   Sunbonnet Sue
Computer Star   Favorite Creatures

GETTING STARTED

Each chapter is divided into three main sections: A narrative about the quilt, directions and diagrams, then patterns and quilting designs.

The narrative tells the personal part of the quilt story, how or why the quilt came to be. It may be a brief sketch about the quilt or its maker, or relate the historical facts or the inspiration for the design. Some of the narratives are anecdotal, with such details as how the quilt got its title or how special people were involved in the making.

The directions are outlined in detail, from start to finish, in six sections: For Starters (vital general information about the quilt), Supplies (fabric), Other Supplies (itemized), Ready to Work (making templates, cutting), Putting It Together (assembly), and The Finishing Touch (quilting and binding). Some of the patterns include a choice of layouts and designs. Some offer an option of construction with scraps or new fabric yardage. Diagrams are concise and given in a step-by-step format so that the beginner, as well as the experienced quilter can follow them.

The last section has full-size patterns and more than twenty original quilting designs.

All this is complemented by full-page color photographs of each quilt. Close-ups of quilting designs and piecing details will help you perfect your patterns, or at least appreciate the ones already executed.

A bibliography of resources for additional ideas is included at the end of the book. The recommended titles are grouped by the quilt pattern name and for general assistance. In them you will find another viewpoint, further options, or in-depth research. Some references are very specific and closely related to the particular quilt pattern. Others are more general in nature, with only small sections that relate to the specific quilt pattern.

So which ones are really my FAVORITE quilts? For sentiment, I'd have to pick the Favorite Creatures Crib Quilt, a mother (me) and son project. For its roots in humble beginnings, the Rice Bag Quilt, a product of my current interest in quilt designs with recycled bags and sacks. For richness of fabrics, the Virginia Reel, a bold mixture of plaids and prints. And finally, for its sheer beauty, and connection to the lifetime of a very dear friend, the French Basket.

Here's hoping you will derive at least a portion of the pleasure that I have from making and/or researching these quilts.

The Quilts

TOKYO, TORONTO, SEOUL, NAIROBI, AND THE AMISH DRY GOODS STORE
(VIRGINIA REEL)
QUILT BY THE AUTHOR

TOKYO, TORONTO, SEOUL, NAIROBI, AND THE AMISH DRY GOODS STORE

A quilt design technique that has captured my interest in the past few years is the use of basic traditional patterns in innovative settings. "Tokyo, Toronto, Seoul, Nairobi, and the Amish Dry Goods Store" is a clear example of how an exceedingly simple block, the Virginia Reel, can be set into an intricate pattern.

Appearing as a printed pattern as early as 1931 in Ruby McKim's *101 Patchwork Patterns*, this familiar four-patch design also answers to names like Snail's Trail, Monkey Wrench, Indiana Puzzle, Interlocking Block, and Whirligig. In its purest graphic form it is simply a box-in-box or square-in-square pattern. Depending on how the fabrics are arranged within the boxes and how the blocks are set together, many design variations from ordinary to chaotic can be explored.

When the blocks are set directly with each other, Virginia Reel creates a classic figure/ground or positive/negative illusion. Squares and triangles come together for a curvilinear effect that resembles the crest of an ocean wave or a spinning whirligig. The resulting interlocking forms mirror each other in a figure/ground illusion, four large triangles joining to form larger squares for a rolling graphic effect.

The set possibilities range from very static (e.g., box-in-box design with separating latticework or alternate plain blocks) to very active (e.g., a mixture of unusual darks and lights in a direct set). Other direct or staggered sets may reveal secondary shapes resembling seahorses, the letter "S," spaceships, or objects and effects reflected by the names Snail's Trail, Whirligig, or Kissing Dinosaurs.

Inspiration for my Virginia Reel adaptation came from two sources: a quilt pictured in the 1984 Quilt Engagement Calendar (Dutton), and a growing accumulation of distinctive bold florals and plaids. I wanted to mix unusual fabrics in a direct set of dark against light, pairing the unlikely combination of plaids and bold florals. My guideline in the selection and pairing of plaids and prints was compatibility, not coordination. Fabrics did not have to "go with each other" in comfy harmony, did not have to be coordinated. Instead, I selected fabrics that were merely compatible, fabrics that were not in disagreement or didn't create jarring contrasts.

The title of the quilt is a reflection of the fabric sources– souvenirs and treasures from my travels, and gifts from quilting pen pals. Fine hand-dyed cotton solids in the border were a gift from a quilting friend in Tokyo. Showy blue, pink, apricot, and green madras plaids are from a specialty goods store in the theatre district of Toronto. Rich bold florals with touches of gold and sea-blue are special purchases at a cotton fabric shop in the heart of Seoul. A coarsely woven cotton "kikoy" plaid from Nairobi found its place in the border. Deep blue, teal, green, and lavender solids from a Wisconsin Amish dry goods store frame the central plaids and prints.

My interest in breaking away from preconceptions while still suggesting the traditional forms is well illustrated in "Tokyo, Toronto, Seoul, Nairobi, and the Amish Dry Goods Store." While the design is based on a familiar pattern, I have elaborated on that familiarity by introducing new concepts in fabric use and exploring new relationships between blocks and borders.

"Tokyo, Toronto, Seoul, Nairobi, and the Amish Dry Goods Store" has become one of my favorite quilts, not so much for design reasons, but for the sentimental feelings, the people, and the impressions it helps recall: a journey to my son's Korean homeland, a "sisters retreat" to Canada, correspondence with a Japanese friend on the opposite side of the globe, an East African excursion, and a trip to the Amish dry goods store.

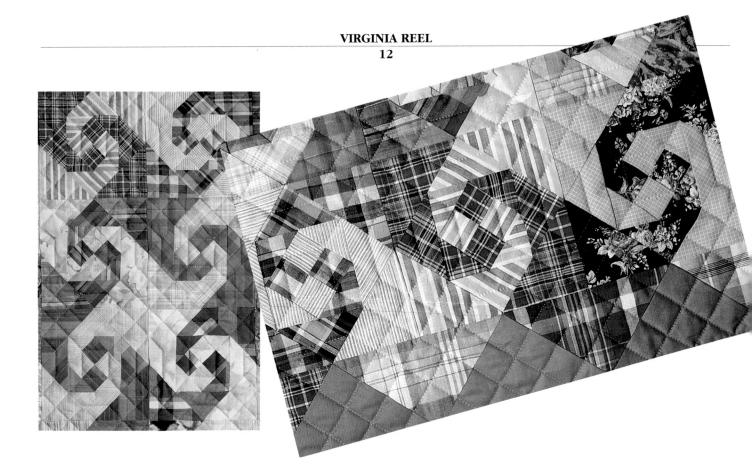

VIRGINIA REEL

FOR STARTERS

The following list will help you enjoy a smooth start and steady progress in your work on the Virginia Reel quilt. It contains a variety of general information about making the quilt:

- Wash and press all fabrics before you begin.
- A minimum of 2 contrasting fabrics is required.
- A mixture of light and dark scrap fabrics works very well. The quilt featured here uses a mixture of plaids and bold prints.
- All seams are ¼ inch.
- For templates (patterns for the quilt pieces) use sturdy plastic, cardboard, or sandpaper, and be sure to note grain lines.
- Piecing may be done by hand or machine. For hand-piecing, make the templates without seam allowances, and add them when marking and cutting the fabrics. For machine-piecing, include ¼" seam allowances on templates.
- Twenty-four (24) pieced blocks are required for this quilt.
- Each pieced block measures 8" square, finished.
- The 4" pieced border is made from the remaining scrap fabrics and a few solid fabrics.
- The finished size for the Virginia Reel quilt is 40" x 56".

SUPPLIES

Use 44"/45" wide cotton or cotton/ polyester blend fabrics.

Quilt Top:

Plaids or stripes: ¼ yard each of 24 fabrics, including both lights and darks, OR 24 pieces of scrap fabrics, minimum size about 12" x 12" .

Bold Prints: Same as plaids and stripes

Solids: A variety of blues, teals, greens, and lavenders, minimum size piece needed about 8" square. A total of 24 pieces are required, but some may be randomly repeated. For new yardage, buy ¼ yard of each of 6 colors.

Binding: 1 yard of deep teal or dark blue

Backing: 1¾ yards of good quality unbleached muslin

Batting: 45" x 60" (crib-size) bonded polyester batt

OTHER SUPPLIES

- Iron
- Material for templates
- Marking pencils or soap chips
- Scissors (for paper and fabric)
- Rulers
- Thread for piecing
- Pins
- Thread or safety pins for basting
- Quilting needles
- 1 spool natural color quilting thread
- Thimble
- Long straightedge
- Hoop or frame for quilting

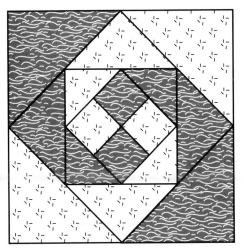

Diagram 1

Diagram 2

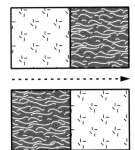

Diagram 3

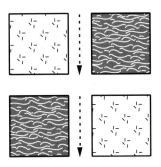

Diagram 4

READY TO WORK

FABRIC KEY

L = Light

D = Dark

S = Solid

TEMPLATES

Begin by making templates of all six Virginia Reel pattern pieces (#1, 2, 3, 4, 5, and 6). Mark the grain lines on each template. It is especially important to note and adhere to grain lines when cutting and piecing triangles. Note that ¼" seams must be added on all sides of each piece.

CUTTING

Begin by separating the 48 plaid and print fabrics into two piles designated Light and Dark. You should have 24 fabrics in each pile. Next, pair a light fabric with a compatible dark fabric, until all fabrics are used. Pin the paired fabrics together.

From EACH of the 48 fabrics, cut the following pieces:

Template #1 (square): Cut 2

Template #2 (triangle): Cut 2

Template #3 (triangle): Cut 2

Template #4 (triangle): Cut 2

From the 48 fabrics, select 6 darks and 10 lights and cut 1 large triangle (Template #5) from each for the pieced border.

Continue with the Solid (S) fabrics and cut the following:

Template #5 (largest triangle): Cut a mixture to total 20

Template #6 (parallelogram): Cut a mixture to total 8 (cut 4 Reverse)

PUTTING IT TOGETHER

BLOCK PIECING

Refer to the Virginia Reel illustration in Diagram 1. Collect the 16 light and dark pieces needed to complete a block. Place the pieces right side up on a flat surface, according to Diagram 1.

Begin by piecing the light and

dark squares together, according to Diagram 2.

Complete the center four-patch as in Diagram 3.

Attach small triangles (2L and 2D) on each side of the pieced center squares, according to Diagram 4. Check to be certain that the light and dark fabrics are properly placed.

Next, attach the medium triangles according to Diagram 5.

Add the outer triangles to complete the 8" block, as illustrated in Diagram 1.

Make a total of twenty-four (24) blocks.

ASSEMBLY

Lay out your blocks on a large flat surface and arrange them according to your color and fabric preferences. Place them with the large triangles coming together to form dark and light "whirligig" shaped clusters, as in Diagram 6. (Also see illustration on page 17, top right.)

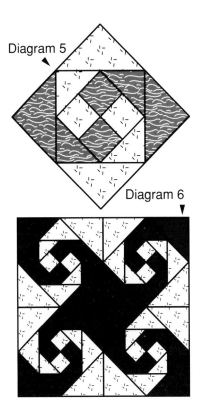

Diagram 5

Diagram 6

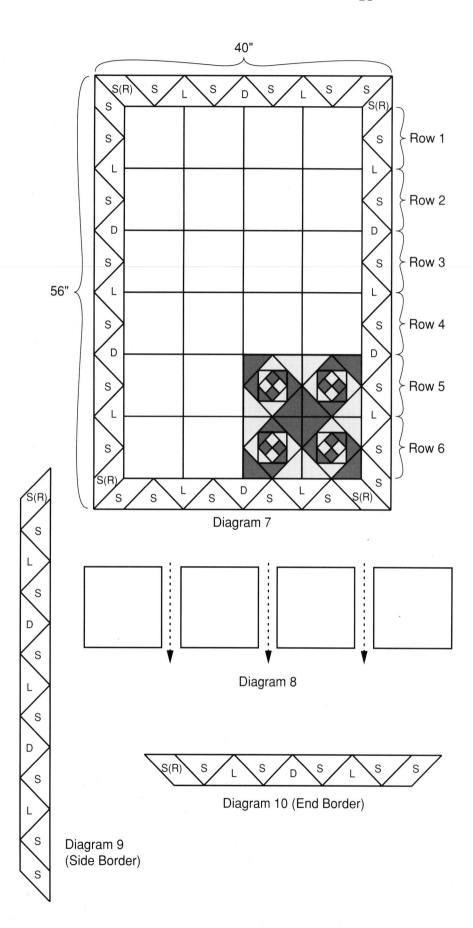

Diagram 7

Diagram 8

Diagram 10 (End Border)

Diagram 9
(Side Border)

Continue to arrange and rearrange with 4 blocks across and 6 blocks down, according to Diagram 7. Fabrics and blocks may be grouped by color or style.

After you have decided on block placement, begin piecing Row 1 in short vertical seams, according to Diagram 8. Piece Rows 2 through 6 in a similar fashion.

Next, join the rows by sewing longer horizontal cross seams, to complete the quilt top center (refer to Diagram 7).

BORDER PIECING

Refer to Diagram 7 and arrange the large plaid triangles and solid triangles and parallelograms around the pieced center.

Begin with the side borders. Piece 3 Light (L) triangles, 2 Dark (D) triangles, 6 Solid (S) triangles, and 2 Solid (S) parallelograms according to Diagram 9. Make 2 side borders.

Refer to Diagram 10 for the top and bottom pieced borders: 2 Light (L) triangles, 1 Dark (D) triangle, 4 Solid (S) triangles, and 2 Solid (S) parallelograms. Make 2 end borders.

Attach the side and end borders to the pieced center, mitering the corners, to complete the quilt top.

THE FINISHING TOUCH

QUILTING

Place the 1¾ yard muslin backing fabric right side down on a large flat surface. Smooth the batting over it. Place the pressed quilt top over the batting, right side up. Pin or thread baste the three layers together for quilting.

Using a washable marker or soap chips and straightedge, mark quilting lines as suggested in Diagram 11, page 15 top. Use natural color quilting thread to quilt along all marked lines.

BINDING

Trim the batting to ½" larger than the quilt top, to allow for filler in the binding. Trim the backing to match the top. From the 1 yard of deep teal or dark blue binding fabric, make 3" wide continuous bias binding.

Fold the binding in half lengthwise, wrong sides together. Then attach it to the quilt front in a seam that penetrates all the layers. Turn the binding to the back of the quilt and whipstitch it in place.

Diagram 11
(Four Block Corner & Border)

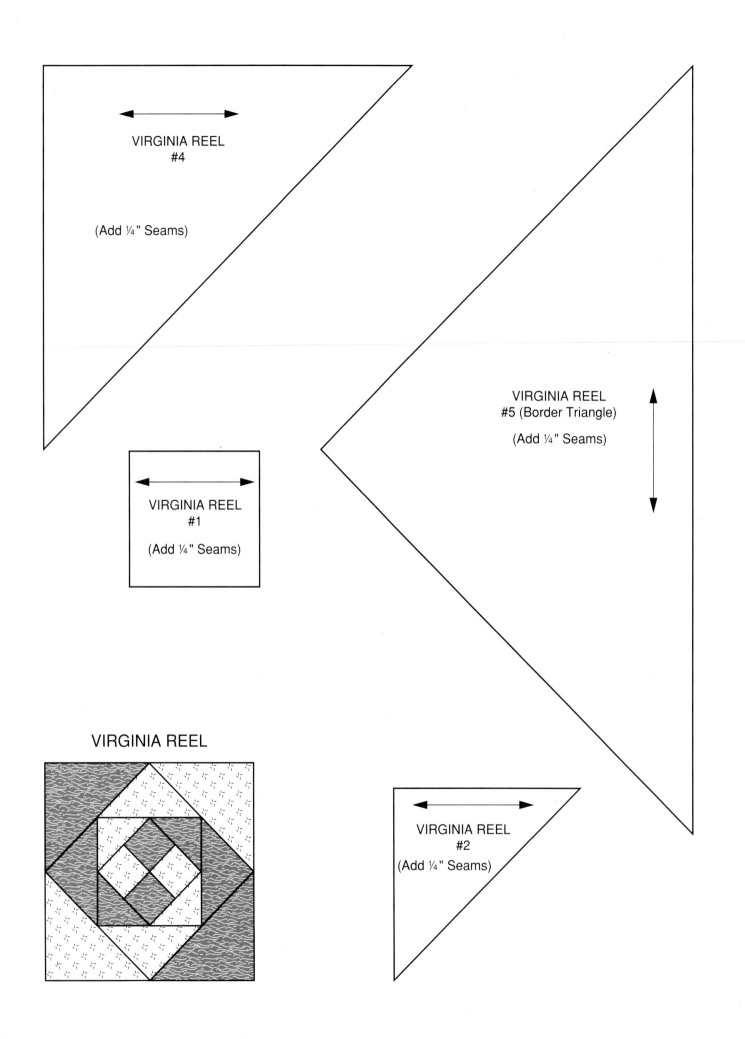

VIRGINIA REEL
#4

(Add ¼" Seams)

VIRGINIA REEL
#5 (Border Triangle)

(Add ¼" Seams)

VIRGINIA REEL
#1

(Add ¼" Seams)

VIRGINIA REEL

VIRGINIA REEL
#2
(Add ¼" Seams)

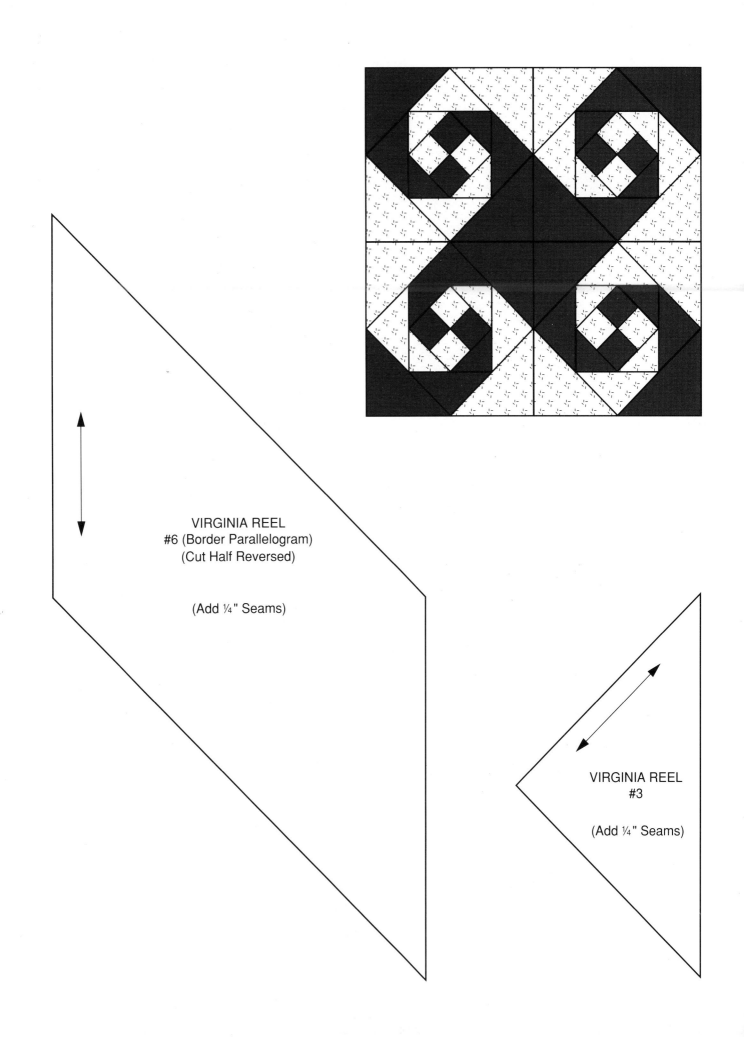

VIRGINIA REEL
#6 (Border Parallelogram)
(Cut Half Reversed)

(Add ¼" Seams)

VIRGINIA REEL
#3

(Add ¼" Seams)

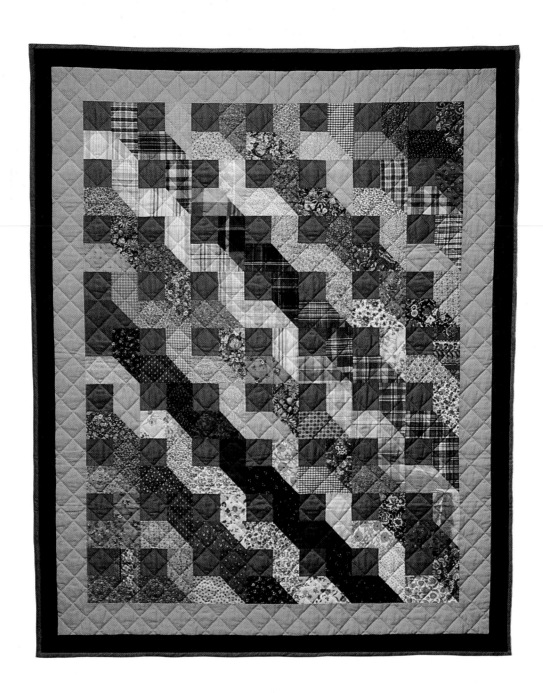

YET ANOTHER VIEW
(ATTIC WINDOWS)
QUILT BY THE AUTHOR

YET ANOTHER VIEW

One of the best things about scrap quilts is that they are most successful when a simple pattern is used. Attic Windows is a good example. It has only two templates (a square and a trapezoid) and only three pieces in each block. The three pieces provide an opportunity to arrange your fabrics in natural groupings of light scraps, dark scraps and solids.

A light scrap and a dark scrap are all that are needed to create an effective two-dimensional design. The addition of a third fabric, such as a solid, produces a feeling of depth, of a third dimension. The result is the illusion of the Attic Window, the feeling of looking out a window, across a room, or from an attic. The third fabric may also function as a unifying factor or color in the quilt design.

Because of its simplicity, Attic Windows can easily be set in numerous design variations and layouts. The way a block is set, that is, how it is placed in relation to the other blocks, latticework, and borders, is a key in the overall design effect, especially with Attic Windows. This phenomenon has been explored and illustrated in my book *Award-Winning Scrap Quilts*. In it I show several set variations, including Traditional, Straight Furrow, Chevron, Skyscraper, Japanese Lantern, and Broken Spools. The settings are taken from my early experiments with the Attic Windows pattern, and they vary from very traditional to entirely random.

A popular alternative approach to the Attic Windows pattern is to feature printed fabrics, objects, or a "view" in the window portion of the block. It has been especially popular to use jungle prints, colorful tropical prints, memorabilia objects, scenic views, bold florals, or even pieced blocks in the "window." This design approach has been researched commendably by Diana Leone in her book *Attic Windows, A Contemporary View*. It is an inspiring resource for anyone interested in in-depth exploration of Attic Windows.

The quilt pictured here is the fourth in my Attic Windows series. It includes a wide range of fabrics — solids, stripes, plaids, hand-painted fabrics, fine calicoes, bold florals, old fabrics from my grandmother's box of scraps, salesperson's swatches, leftovers from home sewing projects, and gift swatches. Fabrics from friends are from places as far apart as North Carolina and British Columbia.

Some fabrics are reversed (placed upside-down). Some diagonal rows are uniformly planned (e.g., all plaids), others involve a variety of fabrics. The result is a mixture that gives the quilt its distinctive character.

My young son David had a part in this Attic Windows quilt. He helped me with thread basting, a task he enjoyed (see the dedication page). I concluded that if he could tolerate, even enjoy, hand basting a quilt, there would be real potential for him as a quiltmaker. I was right. Look elsewhere in this book for the picture and story about the "Favorite Creatures Crib Quilt" that David and I made as a collaborative mother/son project.

ATTIC WINDOWS

FOR STARTERS

The following list will help you enjoy a smooth start and steady progress in your work on the Attic Windows quilt. It contains a variety of general information about making the quilt.

- Wash and press all fabrics before you begin.
- A minimum of 3 fabrics is required: a dark solid, a light print, and a dark print.
- A mixture of scrap fabrics (as many as 125) may be used to create the "windows."
- All seams are ¼".
- For templates (patterns for the quilt pieces) use sturdy plastic, cardboard, or sandpaper, and be sure to note grain lines.

- Piecing may be done by hand or machine. For hand-piecing, make the templates without seam allowances, and add them when marking and cutting fabrics. For machine-piecing, include the ¼" seam allowances on the templates.
- Sixty-three (63) pieced attic windows are needed.
- Each pieced attic window measures 6" x 6", finished.
- Attic Windows may be hung either vertically or horizontally.
- The finished size for Attic Windows is 53" x 65".

SUPPLIES

Use 44"/45" wide cotton or cotton/ polyester blend fabrics.

Quilt Top:

Teal (for squares and binding): 2 yards

Light Scraps: A variety of prints and plaids in mixed colors to total about 2 yards. Minimum scrap size is a rectangle about 4" x 8". If you are buying new fabric, buy ⅛ yard each of several fabrics, up to a total of about 2 yards.

Dark Scraps: Same as Light Scraps

Light Blue (inner borders): 1⅞ yards

Black (outer borders): 2 yards

Binding: (Included in Teal)

Backing: 4 yards of good quality unbleached muslin or a light solid color compatible with the other fabric scraps.

Batting: Use a 72" x 90" (twin-size) bonded polyester batt

OTHER SUPPLIES

- Iron
- Material for templates
- Marking pencils or soap chips
- Scissors (for paper and fabric)
- Rulers
- Dark neutral thread for piecing
- Pins
- Thread or safety pins for basting
- Quilting needles
- 1 spool natural color quilting thread
- Thimble
- Large 45/90 degree plastic triangle
- Long straightedge
- Hoop or frame for quilting

READY TO WORK

COLOR KEY

L= Light Scrap   D= Dark Scrap
T=Teal   LB=Light Blue
B=Black   R=Reverse Template

TEMPLATES

Make sturdy templates from the two Attic Window pattern pieces – a square (#1) and a trapezoid (#2). Mark the grain lines on each template. Note that ¼" seams must be added on all sides of each piece. Template #2 (trapezoid) must be reversed for half of the pieces cut. These reverse pieces are designated

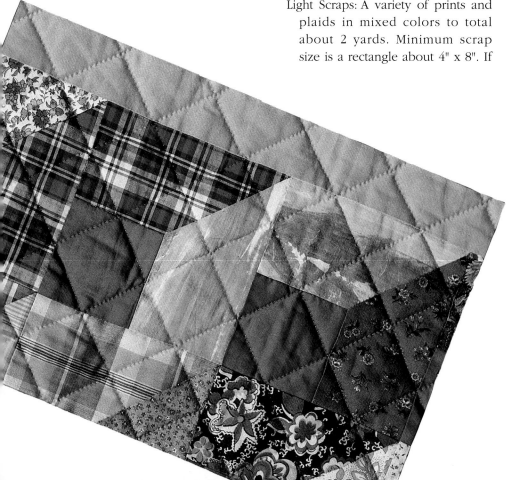

"R" in the instructions and diagrams.

CUTTING

Begin with the Teal (T) fabric. Cut 63 squares from Template #1. Set the remaining Teal fabric aside for binding.

Continue with the Light Scraps (L). Cut a total of 64 trapezoids from Template #2 in a wide range of colors and fabrics. Half of these (32 R) must be cut with the reversed template. You will have one extra Light (L) trapezoid.

Continue with the Dark Scraps (D). Cut a total of 64 trapezoids from Template #2. Half of them (32R) should be cut with the reversed template. You will have one extra Dark (D) trapezoid.

From the Light Blue (LB) fabric, cut the following inner border pieces (allowances for seams and mitering included):

Cut 2 side borders 4" x 61½"

Cut 2 end borders 4" x 49½"

From the Black (B) fabric, cut the following outer border pieces (allowances for seams and mitering included):

Cut 2 side borders 2½" x 65½"

Cut 2 end borders 2½" x 53½"

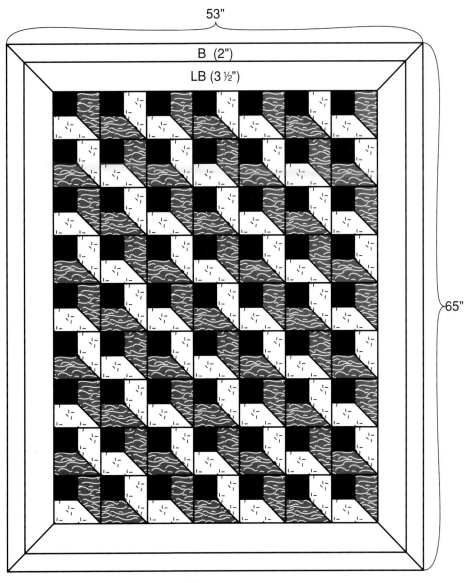

53"

B (2")

LB (3½")

65"

Diagram 1

PUTTING IT TOGETHER

DESIGN DECISIONS

Lay all the cut pieces right side up on a large flat surface, similar to the layout in Diagram 1. Place the Light and Dark fabrics so they form diagonal "ribbons" or "rays of light" across the quilt, reminiscent of the straight furrow variation of the log cabin pattern. Experiment with arrangements that allow the fabrics to give the three-dimensional "window" effect and the diagonal "light and dark" effect.

When you have settled on a design, group the pieces into 63 six-inch units, each consisting of a teal square, a light trapezoid, and a dark trapezoid, as in Diagram 2. Half of these groupings will have the dark and light trapezoids in opposite positions.

BLOCK PIECING

To assemble, begin with the upper left corner of the quilt. Piece a Teal square (T) to light trapezoid (L), as in Diagram 3. Then join the dark (D) trapezoid in a pivot seam, as indicated by the arrows in Dia-

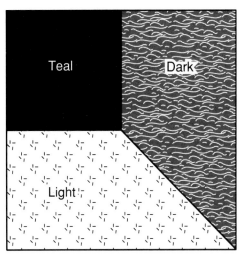

Teal   Dark

Light

Diagram 2

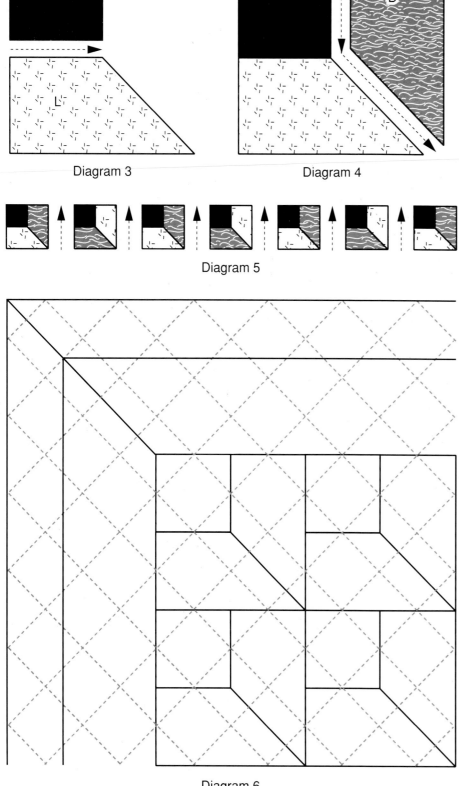

Diagram 3

Diagram 4

Diagram 5

Diagram 6
(Four Block Corner & Border)

gram 4. Press the seams to one side.

Continue across the top row and complete the remaining 6 attic window units that comprise Row 1.

Join the 7 blocks for Row 1 in short vertical seams, as shown in Diagram 5.

Piece the remaining 8 rows in a similar fashion. Then join the 9 rows in long horizontal cross seams.

BORDERS

Use Diagram 1 as your guide. Add the inner Light Blue (LB) borders, mitering corners. Last, attach the outer Black (B) borders, with mitered corners.

THE FINISHING TOUCH

QUILTING

From the 4 yards of backing fabric, cut two 2-yard lengths. Keep one intact (about 42" wide). From the other piece, cut two 10" widths. Join a 10" width to each side of the intact center panel. Press the seams toward the outside.

Place the quilt backing right side down on a large flat surface. Smooth the batting over it. Place the pressed quilt top over the batting, right side up. Pin or thread baste the three layers together for quilting.

With a straightedge or large 45/90° triangle, mark diagonal crosshatch quilting lines as shown in Diagram 6. Hand quilt in natural color quilting thread.

BINDING

Trim the batting to ½" larger than the quilt top, to allow for filler in the binding. Trim the backing to match the top. From the remaining Teal (T) fabric, make 3" wide continuous bias binding.

Fold the binding in half lengthwise, wrong sides together. Then attach it to the quilt front in a seam that penetrates all the layers. Turn the binding to the back and whipstitch it in place.

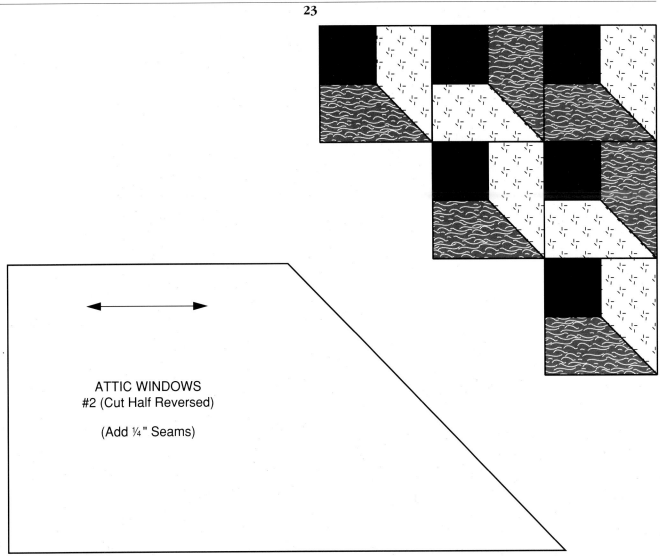

ATTIC WINDOWS

ATTIC WINDOWS
#2 (Cut Half Reversed)

(Add ¼" Seams)

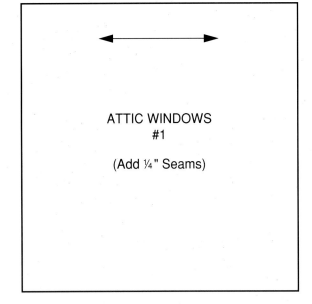

ATTIC WINDOWS
#1

(Add ¼" Seams)

HEAVENLY INSPIRATION
(LONE STAR)
From The Collection Of Maggie Gustafson, Eau Claire, Wisconsin

HEAVENLY INSPIRATION

In popularity, the Lone Star quilt ranks near the top. Drawing inspiration from the heavens, quiltmakers through the centuries have transformed stars into beautiful quilt designs – Blazing Star, Star of Bethlehem, Broken Star, Feathered Star, Sawtooth Star, LeMoyne Star. One of the most widely known is the striking Lone Star.

While stars and their variations have been used for many decades during the 19th and 20th centuries, they continue in popularity. Entire books have been devoted to star patterns and construction techniques, especially the innovative stream-line cutting and assembly methods applicable to new fabric yardages.

Star quilts such as the one shown here, formed from several small diamonds, may appear difficult to piece. They are. Precision piecing and cutting are very important, whether done by hand or machine, because any error will be multiplied as the pieces are joined together into larger units.

Most "older" star quilts, like this one, are made from scraps of fabric. It is unusual to find an older star quilt made of all new fabrics. More commonly they are a mixture of scraps like this one. Diamonds could be cut out from small pieces of leftover fabrics, allowing quilters to use up what they had on hand.

This Lone Star quilt was probably pieced during the 1930's or 1940's. The pieced top came into the possession of Maggie Gustafson from a family member. The nostalgic mixture of fine prints, vivid colors, and naive charm all add up to a pleasing arrangement.

Maggie's Star quilt breaks one common practice. Most makers of multifabric pieced stars, which require both patience and precision to piece, show them off by setting them against a pure white background space with decorative quilting. In this case, the maker used a more subtle soft yellow geometric print to surround her star.

The square Lone Star has been enhanced with a pieced diamond border and elongated by the addition of a wider border panel to the quilt top and bottom. It was hand-quilted in the early 1980's by women in a Wisconsin Amish community. Diamonds are highlighted with simple "V" lines. The background print fabric is embellished with a clever star and circle design. The border features curved feather and heart motifs.

The directions are for a traditional piecing method, by hand or machine, with fabric recommendations that reflect the antique-fabric-mixture feeling of the design. Complete diagrams and quilt motifs are included. You, too, can re-create the stellar charm of this Thirties style quilt.

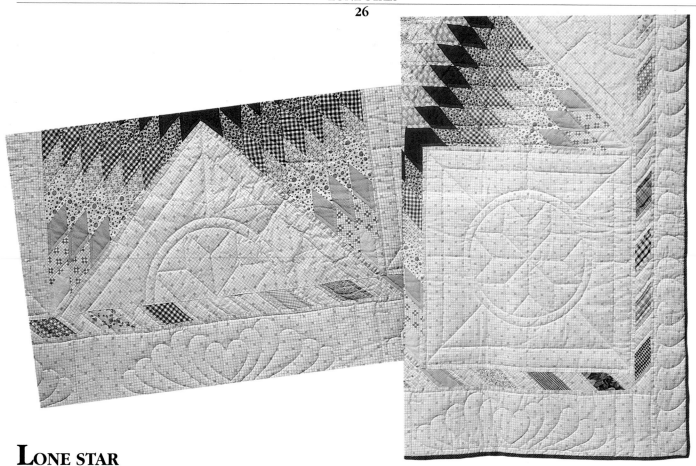

LONE STAR

FOR STARTERS

The following list will help you enjoy a smooth start and steady progress in your work on the Lone Star quilt. It contains a variety of general information about making the quilt.

- Wash and press all fabrics before you begin.
- A minimum of 8 printed fabrics is needed. As many as 15 may be used and are recommended.
- A variety of scrap fabrics may be used for the Lone Star.
- All seams are ¼".
- For the diamond template, use sturdy plastic, cardboard, or sandpaper, and be sure to note grain lines.
- Piecing may be done by hand or machine. For hand-piecing, make the templates without seam allowances, and add them when marking and cutting the fabrics. For machine-piecing, include the

¼" seam allowances on the templates.

- Only one template is required: a 45° diamond that is finished 2½" on each side.
- Suggested fabric amounts listed below are based on a design exactly like the one pictured, which includes one repeated color (gold).
- The finished size for the Lone Star quilt is 77¼" x 83¼".

SUPPLIES

Use 44"/45" wide cotton or cotton/ polyester blend fabrics.

Quilt top fabrics:

Prints: Suggested fabric amounts are listed by concentric stars beginning at the middle of the star and reading out. Note that Fabric #4 and #13 are the same. If you choose to use a different fabric for #13, you will need ⅜ yard of it.

Fabric 1	Dark pink print	¼ yd.
Fabric 2	Light pink print	⅜ yd.
Fabric 3	Green print	⅜ yd.
Fabric 4	Gold solid	¾ yd.
Fabric 5	Yellow print	⅝ yd.
Fabric 6	White print	¾ yd.
Fabric 7	Pink	⅞ yd.
Fabric 8	Red solid	1 yd.
Fabric 9	Pink print	⅞ yd.
Fabric 10	Brown gingham	¾ yd.
Fabric 11	Lavender print	⅝ yd.
Fabric 12	Lavender polka dot	½ yd.
Fabric 13	Gold solid included in #4 above	
Fabric 14	Orange print	⅜ yd.
Fabric 15	Yellow solid	¼ yd.

You may use a variety of scraps in place of any of the above yardages. Note that you will need varying amounts of scraps, ranging from about ¼ yard to one yard.

Background Print: 3¾ yards of a fine print in a color compatible with the star fabrics

Binding: 1 yard of red

Backing: 5¼ yards of good quality unbleached muslin

Batting: Use an 81" x 96" (double size) bonded polyester batt

OTHER SUPPLIES

• Iron
• Material for templates
• Marking pencils or soap chips
• Rulers
• Thread for piecing
• Pins
• Tissue paper or other lightweight paper for patterns
• Thread or safety pins for basting
• Quilting needles
• 2 spools natural color quilting thread
• Thimble
• Long straightedge
• Hoop or frame for quilting

READY TO WORK

FABRIC KEY

Numbers 1 through 15 indicate print fabrics in the star. Letters "A" through "H" indicate Rows for the star assembly.

TEMPLATES

Begin by making a sturdy template of the diamond shown in Diagram 1. Mark the grain line on the template. Note that ¼" seams must be added on all sides.

Next, make a tissue paper pattern for the two background pieces — a large square and a large triangle — shown in Diagram 2 and 3. The indicated measurements are for the finished pattern. Seam allowances must be added on all sides.

CUTTING

Begin with the Print fabrics. The number of diamonds to cut from each fabric is listed next. Note that Fabrics #4 and #13 are the same. If you choose to use a separate fabric for #13, cut 24 of it.

Fabric 1 –   Cut 8
Fabric 2 –   Cut 16
Fabric 3 –   Cut 24
Fabric 4 –   Cut 56 (includes Fabric #13)
Fabric 5 –   Cut 40
Fabric 6 –   Cut 48
Fabric 7 –   Cut 56
Fabric 8 –   Cut 64
Fabric 9 –   Cut 56
Fabric 10 –   Cut 48
Fabric 11 –   Cut 40
Fabric 12 –   Cut 32
Fabric 13 –   (included with Fabric #4)
Fabric 14 –   Cut 16
Fabric 15 –   Cut 8

From the remaining print fabrics cut an additional variety of 60 diamonds to be used in the pieced border.

Continue with the Background Fabric and cut the following borders:

Cut 2 side borders 3½" x 71¾" (seam included)

Cut 2 end borders 6½" x 77¾" (seam included)

Next, cut 4 squares and 4 triangles from the enlarged patterns. Be sure to note the grain lines and add seam allowances all around.

Then cut 60 diamonds to be used in the pieced borders.

PUTTING IT TOGETHER

STAR PIECING

Refer to Diagram 4 for a general layout of the Lone Star. The star is composed of 8 large diamond sections, surrounded by a narrow pieced diamond border and wide outer border.

Construction begins with the large sections of the star. Refer to Diagram 5, page 28, for arrangement of a diamond section (⅛ of the large star). Lay the diamonds (Fabrics #1 through #15) on a flat

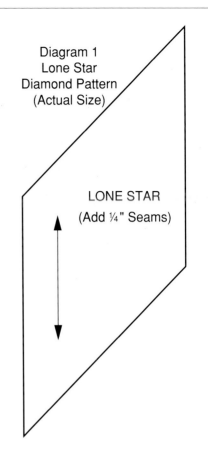

Diagram 1
Lone Star
Diamond Pattern
(Actual Size)

LONE STAR
(Add ¼" Seams)

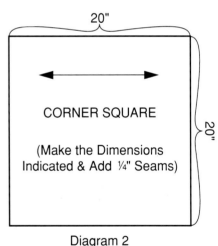

20"

CORNER SQUARE

(Make the Dimensions Indicated & Add ¼" Seams)

20"

Diagram 2

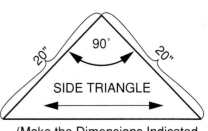

20"   90°   20"

SIDE TRIANGLE

(Make the Dimensions Indicated & Add ¼" Seams)

Diagram 3

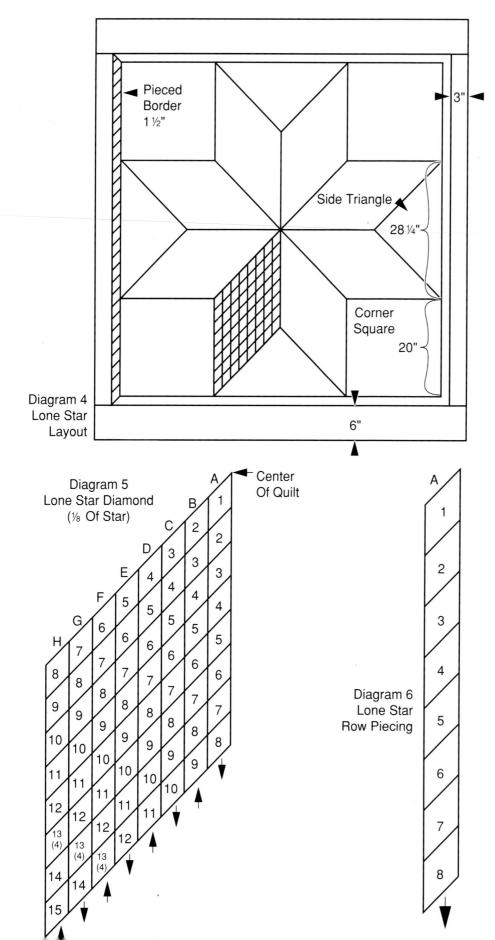

Diagram 4
Lone Star
Layout

Pieced
Border
1 ½"

3"

Side Triangle

28 ¼"

Corner
Square

20"

6"

Diagram 5
Lone Star Diamond
(⅛ Of Star)

Center
Of Quilt

Diagram 6
Lone Star
Row Piecing

surface according to the diagram. Each segment has a total of 64 pieces.

Begin piecing with Row A (Fabrics #1 through #8). Collect the 8 diamonds. Piece these together in ¼" seams, as shown in Diagram 6. Press the seams all in one direction, as suggested by the arrow.

Continue piecing with Row B (Fabrics #2 through #9). Press the seams in Row B in the opposite direction, as indicated by the arrow in Diagram 5. Continue piecing Rows C, D, E, F, G, and H, pressing each row in an alternate direction.

Next, join all 8 rows to complete the large diamond section.

Lay the completed diamond sections in a star arrangement. Then piece the sections together according to the three steps illustrated in Diagram 7.

Next, add the large corner squares and side triangles, matching and pinning at all corners. Use pivot seams as suggested by the arrows in Diagram 8.

PIECED BORDERS

The narrow pieced border is made from diamonds, alternating between the print fabrics and the background fabric. Piece 30 diamonds (15 various prints and 15 background) in a fashion similar to the first step in the star piecing (Diagram 6). The length of the pieced strip will be about 75 inches. Make 4 border strips and stitch one to each side of the pieced top.

OUTER BORDERS

To complete the Lone Star quilt top, add the 3" side borders and then the 6" top and bottom borders, as shown in Diagram 4.

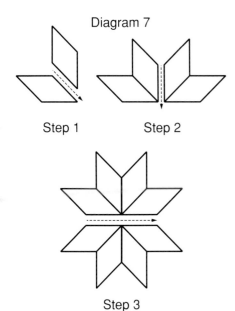

Diagram 7

Step 1   Step 2

Step 3

Diagram 8

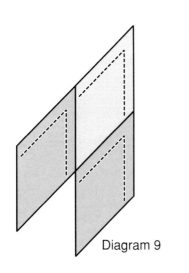

Diagram 9

THE FINISHING TOUCH

QUILTING

From the 5¼ yards of unbleached muslin, cut two, 2⅝ yard lengths. Keep one intact (about 42" wide). From the other piece, cut two 21" widths. Join a 21" width to each side of the intact center panel. Press seams toward the outside.

Place the quilt backing right side down on a large flat surface. Smooth the batting over it. Place the pressed quilt top over the batting, right side up. Pin or thread baste the three layers together for quilting.

Use a washable marker to mark the following quilting designs. Use natural color quilting thread.

•On each diamond in the star, quilt ¼" from the seams on two adjacent sides, forming a "V" shape, as shown in Diagram 9.

•Quilt the suggested design in Diagram 10 (to be enlarged) in the 4 large background squares. Use ½ of the design (divided diagonally) for the 4 side triangles.

•Quilt the narrow pieced border as suggested in Diagram 11.

•Quilt the feather design (Design A) on the top and bottom (6") borders. Note that this is only one-half of the design and it must be folded over to create the full-size pattern. Place 3 of these designs on each end. Add 3 parallel lines, each about 1½" apart, to fill the area between the designs.

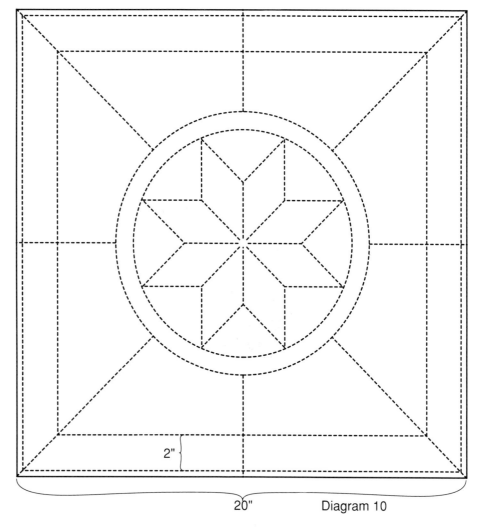

2"

20"   Diagram 10

• Quilt the modified heart design (Design B) on the side (3") borders. Note that this is only one-half of the design and the quilting pattern must be folded over to create the full-size pattern. Center one on each side. For the remaining 4 designs, extend the pattern by adding 3 more hearts to each end. Quilt parallel lines, about 1½" apart to fill the area between the designs.

BINDING

Trim the batting to ½" larger than the quilt top to allow for filler in the binding. Trim the backing to match the top. From the one yard of red binding fabric, make 3" wide continuous bias binding.

Fold the binding in half lengthwise, wrong sides together. Then attach it to the quilt front in a seam that penetrates all the layers. Turn the binding to the back and whipstitch it in place.

Diagram 11
Suggested Quilting
for Pieced Border

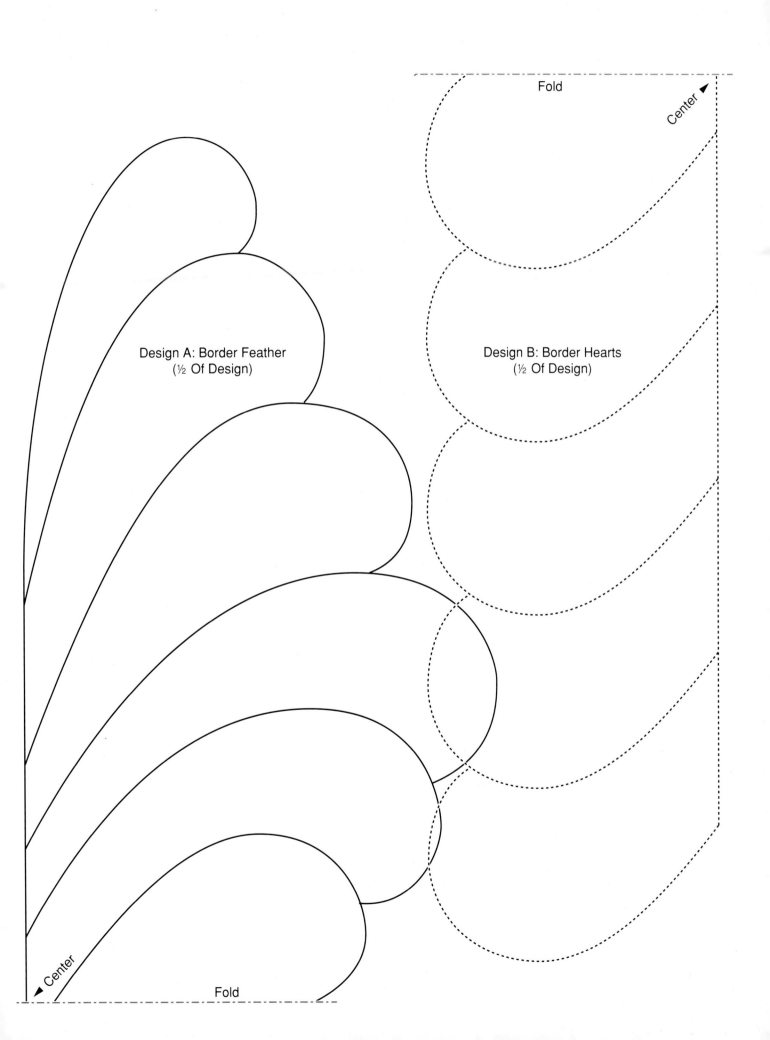

Fold

Center

Design A: Border Feather
(½ Of Design)

Design B: Border Hearts
(½ Of Design)

Center

Fold

A HODGEPODGE OF FABRICS AND FRIENDS
(FOUR-PATCH ALBUM)
BLOCKS BY CHIPPEWA COUNTY FRIENDS,
COMPLETED AND QUILTED BY THE AUTHOR

A HODGEPODGE OF FABRICS AND FRIENDS

The four-patch Album block is a popular pattern choice for friendship signature quilts. Also known as Chimney Sweep, Album Patch, Friendship Chain, or Courthouse Square, its diagonal set forms a center rectangle or cross in which names, dates, or other information may be inscribed.

The blocks in this Album quilt were made by twelve of my Chippewa County friends – Debbie Peterson, Muriel Boyken, Margaret Schoenberg, Joyce Sperber, Gerry Hutton, Marky Kuba, Judy Gaier, Ione Hurt, Eileen Vodacek, Jan Newmann, Sue Sorum, and Phyllis Vetterkind. They have been students in my quilting classes for many semesters.

During a recent Scrap Quilting course, we explored the use of traditional patterns in fabric mixture quilts. The Album pattern was one we studied, for its adaptability to scrap use and its suitability for memory style quilts. At the end of the course, my students presented a collection of Album blocks in a carefully fashioned fabric covered box to me. It was a thoughtful and generous gesture that confirmed all the good feelings among the class participants. Each 12" block was signed, in embroidery, cross-stitch, or ink. Some used first names, some used names and initials, some used nicknames. Some were in block style, some cursive. Some were dated. Each block was a mixture of fabrics and choice of colors that reflected the individuality of its maker.

That was in 1986. For nearly two years I contemplated the collection, taking the box down from the shelf and carefully admiring the hodgepodge of fabrics and recalling the good times with quilt friends. Then I would re-stack the blocks in the box and return it to its special shelf.

Eventually, I could no longer justify my procrastination, and I became determined to face my dilemma. How was I to arrange twelve blocks made from diverse fabrics, in a wide spreading color range, and with no coordination among the blocks (some had a cross-shaped space for the inscription while others merely had a rectangle).

I considered several setting options – from very traditional to possibly eclectic. First I tried a light muslin background. Ordinary, at best. Then I tried a dark solid background. Not remarkable. Next I tried a fine print background. Just barely satisfactory. I thought I had exhausted the possibilities when it dawned on me that I could continue the theme of multi-fabrics into the background squares and triangles. I searched my fabric collection for a range of prints – fine, medium and bold – compatible with the already dissimilar blocks. I considered dozens of fabrics, accepting, rejecting, and rearranging yardages and blocks in what initially felt like a hit and miss procedure.

Eventually I confirmed that this last option – mixed fabrics in the background, as well – afforded the best opportunity to orchestrate the assortment of colors into a homogeneous composition. Blocks with a touch of blue are clustered near the upper left corner, green and teal fabrics near the upper right. Neutrals of gold, tan, and brown gravitate to the lower left, roses and burgundy to the lower right. Six fine background prints are placed in the six center squares (set on point), encompassing the light color Album blocks. Darker and bolder prints (and a token plaid) appear in the outer triangles. The piece is bound in navy blue.

Decisions about how and where to hand quilt were easier to make. Generally I followed a guideline of placing quilting lines at opposite angles to the threads (grain lines) of the fabric pieces. My choice was straight and diagonal lines, to produce optimum and uniform relief and shadowing.

A label, lovingly hand-stitched by Margaret S., is displayed on the back of the quilt.

FOUR-PATCH ALBUM FRIENDSHIP SIGNATURE QUILT

FOR STARTERS

The following list will help you enjoy a smooth start and steady progress in your work on the Friendship quilt. It contains a variety of general information about making the quilt:

- Wash and press all fabrics before you begin.
- A mixture of scrap print fabrics is an excellent choice for this friendship quilt.
- Names may be inscribed with embroidery thread or permanent pen.
- All seams are ¼".
- For templates (patterns of the quilt pieces) use sturdy plastic, cardboard, or sandpaper, and be sure to note grain lines.
- Piecing may be done by hand or machine. For hand-piecing, make the templates without seam allowances, and add them when marking and cutting the fabrics. For machine-piecing, include the ¼"-wide seam allowance on the templates.
- Twelve (12) pieced blocks are required.
- Each pieced block measures 12" x 12", finished.
- Alternate blocks and background triangles are cut from a mixture of 20 scrap fabrics.
- The finished size for the Friendship quilt is 51" x 68".

SUPPLIES

Use 44"/45" wide cotton or cotton/ polyester blend fabrics.

Quilt Top:

Medium or Dark Prints (for pieced blocks): 12 fabrics, ¼ yard each, OR 12 pieces of scrap fabric, minimum size about 12" x 16".

White or Unbleached Muslin (for pieced blocks); 1½ yards

Medium or Dark Prints (for alternate blocks and side and corner triangles):

For the 6 alternate blocks in the center – 6 fabrics, ½ yard each, OR 6 pieces of scrap fabric, minimum size about 14" x 14".

For the 10 side triangles – 10 fabrics, ¼ yard each, OR 10 pieces of scrap fabrics, minimum size about 20" x 20".

For the 4 corner triangles – 4 fabrics, ¼ yard each, OR 4 pieces of scrap fabric, minimum size about 10" x 10".

Binding: 1 yard of navy blue fabric.

Backing: 4¼ yards of good quality unbleached muslin

Batting: 72" x 90" (twin-size) bonded polyester batt

OTHER SUPPLIES

- Iron
- Material for templates
- Marking pencils or soap chips
- Scissors (for paper and fabric)
- Rulers
- Thread for piecing
- Pins
- Embroidery floss
- Thread or safety pins for basting
- Quilting needles
- 2 spools natural color quilting thread
- Thimble
- Long straightedge
- Hoop or frame for quilting
- Tissue paper for patterns
- (Optional) Permanent pen for name inscriptions

READY TO WORK

COLOR AND FABRIC KEY

W= White or Unbleached Muslin

P= Prints

TEMPLATES

Note: These instructions assume the use of only one print fabric in each block. Several of the blocks in the photographed quilt use MORE than one print per block. This enriches the block designs. You may include as many as 4 or 5 prints in each block. If 2 prints are used, one print for the squares and the other print for the rectangles is a good design alternative.

Begin by making templates of all seven Friendship quilt pattern pieces (1, 2, 3, 4, 5, 6, and 7). Mark the grain lines on each template. Note that ¼" seams must be added on all sides of each piece. Note that patterns 5, 6, and 7 must be drawn larger. Because of their large size, it may be easier to make only paper patterns of 5, 6, and 7. Make the customary cardboard or plastic templates for 1, 2, 3, and 4.

CUTTING

Begin with the White (W) fabric (or unbleached muslin). Cut the following background pieces for the blocks:

Template #1 (square): Cut 24

Template #2 (triangle): Cut 144

Template #3 (triangle): Cut 48

Template #4 (rectangle): Cut 12

Note the suggested grain lines, especially on the triangle templates, as these form the outer edge of each pieced block.

Continue with the Print (P) fabrics for the 12 pieced blocks. From EACH fabric, you need to cut the following:

Template 1 (square): Cut 8

Template 4 (rectangle): Cut 4

Next, cut the 6 large blocks (Template 5, to be drawn larger) from the appropriate medium and dark print fabrics. See unnumbered squares in Diagram 6, page 37. Each square will measure 12½" x 12½" with seam allowances.

Cut the 10 side triangles with Template 6 (drawn larger) as your guide. Note the suggested grain lines and add seams all around.

Last, cut the 4 corner triangles with Template 7 (drawn larger) as your guide. Be sure to note grain lines and add seams.

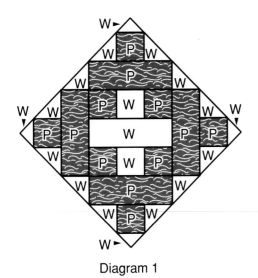

Diagram 1

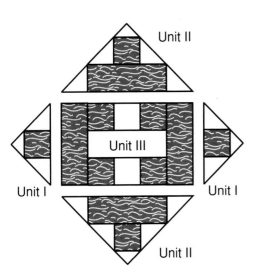

Diagram 2

Diagram 3
Unit I (Make 2)

Diagram 4
Unit II (Make 2)

PUTTING IT TOGETHER

BLOCK PIECING

Refer to the Friendship block illustration in Diagram 1. Collect the 31 pieces needed to complete a block: 10 squares (2 white, 8 print), 12 white large triangles, 4 white small triangles, and 5 rectangles (1 white, 4 print). Place the pieces right sides up on a flat surface as in Diagram 1.

The Friendship block is composed of 3 different construction units, as shown in Diagram 2, to be completed in the following steps:

• For Unit I (shown in Diagram 3) piece large white (W) triangles on opposite sides of a print (P) square. Then join a small white (W) triangle along the short side. Make 4 such units. Set 2 aside and use 2 for completion of Unit II.

• For Unit II (shown in Diagram 4) piece 2 large white (W) triangles on opposite sides of a print (P) rectangle. Attach this to the long side of a completed Unit I. Make 2 of Unit II.

• For Unit III (shown in Diagram 5) piece print (P) squares on each side of the white (W) squares. Add

the white (W) rectangle between them. Then join a print (P) rectangle to each side to complete Unit III.

• Refer to Diagram 2 to complete the Friendship block. Join a Unit I to each end of the central Unit III. Then join a Unit II to the top and bottom. The block will be 12" x 12" plus seam allowances.

• Make a total of twelve (12) blocks.

• Inscribe names in the blocks with embroidery floss or permanent pen.

ASSEMBLY

Refer to Diagram 6 for the general layout of the quilt top. Decisions regarding placement of your blocks must be made now. Lay out your 12 blocks on a large flat surface and arrange them according to your plan or preference. Number each block with a small label, 1 through 12, according to Diagram 6.

Add the 6 alternate background blocks in the center of the quilt. Next, place the 10 side triangles and the 4 corner triangles around the edge of the quilt.

Blocks are assembled in a diagonal fashion, in 6 panels, as

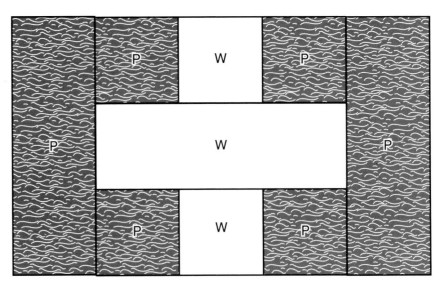

Diagram 5
Unit III (Make 1)

suggested in Diagram 7. Begin with the upper left corner of the quilt. Piece two triangles and a corner triangle around Block 1. Make a similar section with Block 12 for the lower right corner of the quilt.

Next, make a diagonal section with Blocks 2 and 4. Add a large print alternate block between them and a side triangle on each end. Make a similar diagonal section with Blocks 9, and 11, using Diagram 7 as your guide.

Complete the next section by joining Blocks 3, 5, and 7 with 2 large alternate blocks between them, a side triangle on one end (near Block 7), and a corner triangle on the other end (near Block 3). Make a

similar diagonal section with Blocks 6, 8, and 10.

Stitch the six diagonal sections together to complete the quilt top.

THE FINISHING TOUCH

QUILTING

From the 4¼ yards of muslin backing fabric, cut two 2⅛ yard lengths. Keep one intact (about 42" wide). From the other piece, cut two 10" widths. Join a 10" width to each side of the intact center panel. Press seams toward the outside.

Place the quilt backing right side down on a large flat surface. Smooth the batting over it. Place the pressed quilt top over the batting, right side up. Pin or thread baste the three

layers together for quilting.

Using a long straightedge and a washable marking pencil or soap chip, mark the quilting lines and designs suggested in Diagram 8. Quilt along all marked lines, using natural color quilting thread.

BINDING

Trim the batting to ½" larger than the quilt top, to allow for filler in the binding. Trim the backing to match the top. From the 1 yard of navy blue binding fabric, make 3" wide continuous bias binding.

Fold the binding in half lengthwise, wrong sides together. Stitch it to the quilt front in a seam that penetrates all five layers. Turn the binding to the back and whipstitch it in place.

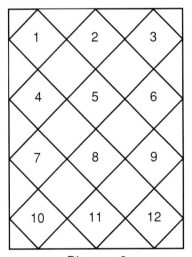

Diagram 6

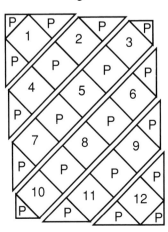

Diagram 7

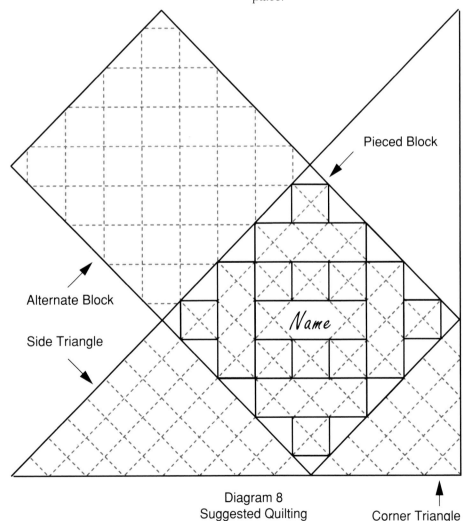

Pieced Block

Alternate Block

Side Triangle

Name

Diagram 8
Suggested Quilting

Corner Triangle

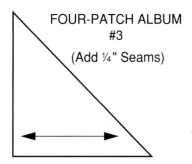

FOUR-PATCH ALBUM
#3

(Add ¼" Seams)

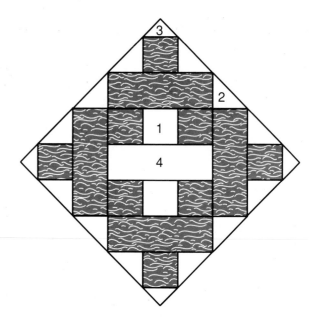

FOUR-PATCH ALBUM

FOUR-PATCH ALBUM
#1

(Add ¼" Seams)

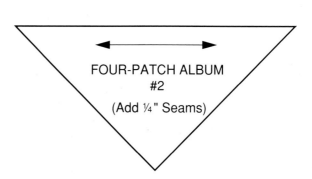

FOUR-PATCH ALBUM
#2

(Add ¼" Seams)

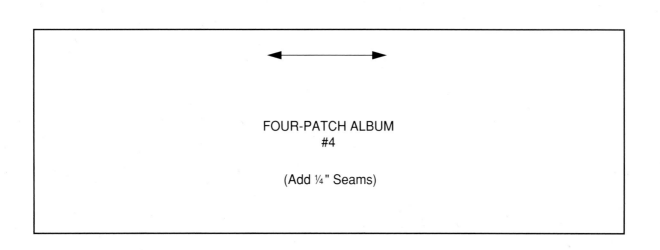

FOUR-PATCH ALBUM
#4

(Add ¼" Seams)

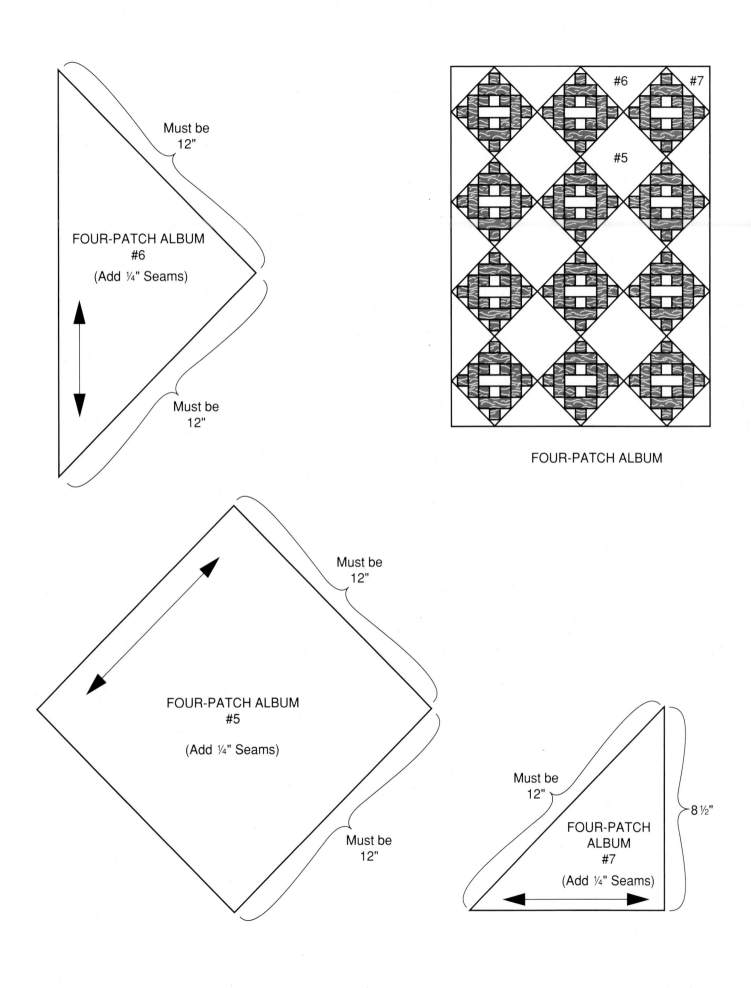

FOUR-PATCH ALBUM
#6

(Add ¼" Seams)

Must be
12"

Must be
12"

#6   #7

#5

FOUR-PATCH ALBUM

FOUR-PATCH ALBUM
#5

(Add ¼" Seams)

Must be
12"

Must be
12"

Must be
12"

8 ½"

FOUR-PATCH
ALBUM
#7

(Add ¼" Seams)

LYDIA A, LULA U, ELSIE G, ET AL.
(ALBUM)
From The Collection Of Sue Terman, Eau Claire, Wisconsin

LYDIA A, LULA U, ELSIE G, ET AL.

The Birthday Club Album Quilt was first called to my attention in 1977. Our local University Quiltmakers were preparing for our first quilt show. Quilts were solicited from among our members, other University personnel, and community members. My friend Erma Terman told me about her mother's 1939 Birthday Club Quilt. She invited me to come and see it. I was immediately impressed with the quilt and its history.

We hung the quilt in our 1978 show. It was a favorite among the viewers. The thirty-one bold album blocks and the inscriptions of names, date, and location lent a personal touch. Viewers studied the quilt with a sense of wonder and curiosity about these twenty-six women, about what their life in 1939 might have been like. Each name carried the ring of a generation past, a reminder of one's own mother, grandmother, or aunt. Wouldn't you like to meet and talk with Adelia H or Lula U, or Ottelia H?

The maker of the 1939 Birthday Club Quilt was Erma Terman's mother, Lydia Yankee Anding (both now deceased). The quilt was made in the Township of Lynn in Clark County, near Neillsville, Wisconsin. Additional information regarding the quilt was secured from Elsie Short (one of the three *Elsie's* inscribed on the quilt) who is now well into her nineties and still resides in the Lynn Township area. Her clear and detailed recollections are documented in a birthday club scrapbook (complete with photographs, newspaper clippings, and memorabilia) that she maintains to this day, even though the club is not nearly as active or as large as in past years.

Here are some of Elsie's recollections: This quilt is one of twenty-five (25, count 'em) friendship quilts that were made by club members in the late 1930's. All of the quilts incorporated the same Album Friendship block, but the names inscribed on each quilt varied slightly, to include personal family members. One woman printed all the names on the blocks (bless her soul). Each member put their quilt together with stripping and border fabrics and colors of her choice. Quilting designs also were a personal choice. Several of the quilts were put on a frame and the quilting was started by club members, then completed by the individual members.

The cost for all these quilts? Muslin was 5 cents a yard in 1936 at the Farmer's Store in Neillsville. This is documented on a bill of sale in the scrapbook. Printed fabrics were higher – 8 cents, 10 cents, or 12 cents a yard. A bill of sale for the fabric for one quilt totalled less than $5.00.

The names inscribed on the quilt include only the first name and the initial of the last name. The blocks on Lydia Anding's quilt are inscribed with the following names: Maggie J, Lula U, Edna S, Elsie G, Violet W, Leona S, Libby A, Anna M, Selma G, Helen H, Emma A, Elsie S, Elsie G, Lydia A (the maker), Lizzie S, Addie R, Elda B, Ella S, Ottelia H, Adelia H, Laura H, Dorothy C, Etta A, Florence A, Ruby D, and Lillian H.

Several of the Birthday Club members are still living today, well into their eighties and nineties. Lydia's quilt is now in the collection of her grandson's family in Eau Claire, Wisconsin. It is a touching tribute to the women who were the heart of the Lynn Birthday Club.

Complete instructions for this Album-style friendship quilt, including piecing directions and intricate quilting designs, are given on the following pages. These can easily be personalized and adapted to your "friendship" group. Here's hoping you'll capture a portion of the joy and sentiment reflected in the Lynn Birthday Club Album Quilt.

ALBUM QUILT

FOR STARTERS

The following list will help you enjoy a smooth start and steady progress in your work on the Album Quilt. It contains a variety of general information about making the quilt.

- Wash and press all fabrics before you begin.
- A minimum of 3 fabrics is required: a light solid, a dark solid, and a print.
- A mixture of 31 scrap prints is an excellent alternative.
- All seams are ¼".
- For templates (patterns of the quilt pieces) use sturdy plastic, cardboard, or sandpaper, and be sure to note grain lines.
- Piecing may be done by hand or machine. For hand-piecing, make the templates without seam allowances, and add them when marking and cutting the fabrics. For machine-piecing, include the ¼" seam allowances on the templates.
- Thirty-one (31) pieced blocks are required.
- Each pieced block measures 10½" x 10½", finished.
- All latticework, borders, and binding are deep blue.
- The finished size for the Album Quilt is 75¼" x 93¼".

SUPPLIES

Use 44"/45" wide cotton or cotton/ polyester blend fabrics.

Quilt Top:

Light Solid (ecru): 4¼ yards
Medium Prints: ⅛ yard each of 31 prints OR 31 pieces of scrap fabric, minimum size about 12" x 12" square
Dark Solid (royal blue): 5 yards

Binding: Buy an additional 1 yard of the royal blue or a contrasting color of your choice.

Backing: 6 yards of good quality unbleached muslin

Batting: Use an 81" x 96" (double size) bonded polyester batt

OTHER SUPPLIES

- Iron
- Material for templates
- Marking pencils or soap chips
- Scissors (for paper and fabric)
- Rulers
- Thread for piecing
- Pins

- Embroidery floss
- Thread or safety pins for basting
- Quilting needles
- 2 spools natural color quilting thread
- Thimble
- Long straightedge
- Hoop or frame for quilting

READY TO WORK

COLOR KEY
L= Light Solid
P= Print
D= Dark

TEMPLATES

Begin by making templates of all six Album Block pattern pieces (1, 2, 3, 4, 5, and 6). Mark the grain lines on each template. Note that ¼" seams must be added on all sides of each piece. Note that patterns 5 and 6 must be enlarged. Because of their large size, it is easier to make only paper patterns for 5 and 6. Make the customary cardboard or plastic templates for 1, 2, 3, and 4.

CUTTING

Begin with the Light Solid (L) fabric. Cut the following pieces:
Template 1 (square): Cut 62
Template 2 (large triangle): Cut 248
Template 3 (small triangle): Cut 124
Template 4 (rectangle): Cut 31

Be sure to adhere to the grain line suggestions, especially on the triangle pieces, as these form the outer edge of each pieced block and are subject to possible distortion.

Continue with the Print (P) fabrics (or scraps). For each album block you will need to cut 8 squares from Template 1. If you are using the same fabric throughout the quilt, cut a total of 248 squares. If you are using a different fabric or scrap in each block (as in the photographed quilt), you will need to cut 8 each from 31 different fabrics.

Next, cut the following pieces from the Dark Solid (D) fabric, for the latticework and outer border areas:

Latticework (measurements include ¼" seam allowances)
Cut (24) 3" x 11"
Cut (2) 3" x 24"
Cut (2) 3" x 50"
Cut (2) 3" x 76"

Outer Border Area (seam allowances must be added as indicated)
Cut (10) of Template 5 (must be drawn larger), large trapezoids for the sides and ends of the quilt
Cut (4) of Template 6 (must be drawn larger), large corner trapezoids

Refer to Diagram 1 as a guide for shapes and general placement.

PUTTING IT TOGETHER

BLOCK PIECING

Refer to the Album block illustration in Diagram 2. Collect the 23 pieces needed to complete a block: 10 squares (2 light, 8 print), 8 large light triangles, 4 small light triangles, and 1 light rectangle. Place the pieces right side up on a flat surface, according to Diagram 2.

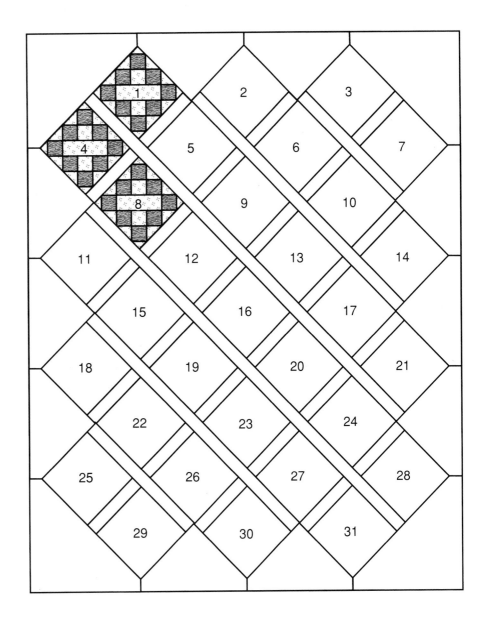

Diagram 1

Diagram 2

Diagram 3
Unit I (Make 4
For Each Block)

Diagram 4
Unit II (Make 1
For Each Block)

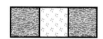

Diagram 5
Piecing For Unit II

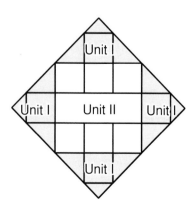

Diagram 6

The Album block is composed of 2 smaller units, to be completed according to the following 5 steps:

• For Unit 1 (show in Diagram 3), piece large (L) triangles on opposite sides of a print (P) square. Then join a small light (L) triangle along the short side. Make 3 more of Unit I, for a total of 4.

• For Unit II (shown in Diagram 4), piece 2 print (P) squares on opposite sides of a light (L) square, according to Diagram 5. Make 2 such panels. Place a light (L) rectangle between the two panels and stitch them to complete Unit II.

• Complete the block by attaching a Unit I on each of the four sides of the central Unit II, according to Diagram 6. The finished block will measure 10½" x 10½" inches.

• Make a total of thirty-one (31) blocks.

• Inscribe names in the blocks with embroidery stitches.

ASSEMBLY OF LATTICEWORK AND BLOCKS:

Short Strips: Refer back to Diagram 1 for the general layout of the quilt top. Note that the latticework is composed of several longer strips (of varied lengths) placed diagonally across the quilt from the top left corner to the lower right corner. Note the placement of the shorter lattice strips in the opposite diagonal directions. Assembly will be in diagonal panels.

Placement of Blocks: Decisions regarding block placement must be made now. Lay your blocks out on a large flat surface and arrange according to your plan or pre-ference. Number each block with a small label, numbers 1 through 31, according to Diagram 1.

Begin by joining Blocks #3 and 7 with a short strip (3" x 11") between them. Be sure that each

block is properly placed with the inscription or name in a readable position. Place this pieced panel back down on the flat surface.

Continue with Blocks 2, 6, 10, and 14. Join these with the three short strips between each block. Set this panel (and all additional panels, as they are pieced) back on the flat surface. In a similar manner, piece the short strips between Blocks 1, 5, 9, 13, 17, and 21.

The longest panel is next – Blocks 4, 8, 12, 16, 20, 24, and 28, – pieced together with six short strips. Continue with the next diagonal panel – Blocks 11, 15, 19, 23, 27, and 31, pieced together with five short strips. The final two panels are Blocks 18, 22, 26, and 30, joined with three short strips, and the short panel consisting of Blocks 25 and 29 joined with one short strip.

LONG STRIPS

Join the diagonal panels together with the longer latticework strips, according to Diagram 7. The shorter strips (3" x 24") are used at the outer corners (lower left and upper right). The long strips (3" x 76") are used in the center area. The medium strips (3" x 50") are placed in the in-between areas.

OUTER BORDER AREAS

To complete the quilt top, add large dark solid (D) side and corner trapezoids (Templates 5 and 6). Begin by joining the 4 corners (Template 6), as in Diagram 8 (seam 1). Then join the 10 end and side trapezoids, using a pivot seam, as shown in Diagram 8 (seams 2 and 3). Match and pin all corners and points before piecing. Stitch according to the suggested arrows in Diagram 8.

Last, stitch the outer short seams (at 14 locations) between the large blue trapezoids, to complete the quilt top (seam 4).

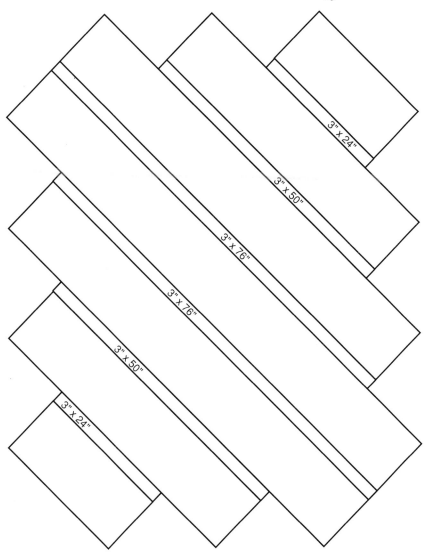

Diagram 7
(Measurements Include Seam Allowances)

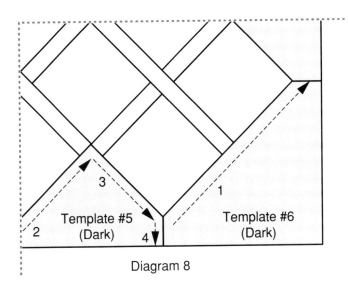

Diagram 8

THE FINISHING TOUCH

QUILTING

From the 6 yards of unbleached muslin, cut two 3 yard lengths. Keep one intact (about 42" wide). From the other piece, cut two 21" widths. Join a 21" width to each side of the intact center panel. Press seams toward the outside.

Place the quilt backing right side down on a large flat surface. Smooth the batting over it. Place the pressed quilt top over the batting, right side up. Pin or thread baste the three layers together for quilting.

Mark the 6 quilting designs in the dark blue latticework and outer areas as follows:

• Mark Quilting Design A (cable) on the 2½" lattices surrounding the blocks. Center the cable with the center of the pieced block.

• Mark Quilting Design B (four point star) in the corner areas between the blocks, where the strips and lattices meet.

• Mark Quilting Design C (large feathered circle) in the center of each corner trapezoid (Template 6).

• Place a Quilting Design D (swirls/square) on the corner trapezoids on either side of Design C, to best fit the corner territory.

• Place Quilting Design E (large feathered teardrop) in the center of each side and end trapezoid (Template 5).

• Place a Quilting Design F (small flower) on the side and end trapezoids, on either side of Design E to best fit the territory.

Quilt along all marked lines, using natural quilting thread.

Also quilt ¼" from the seam lines (inside and outside) on all the pieces in the Album Block, as suggested in Diagram 9. Add a line of quilting around each block, ¼" from the seams.

BINDING

Trim the batting to ½" larger than the quilt top, to allow for filler in the binding. Trim the backing to match the top. From the additional (or remaining) 1 yard of royal blue or contrasting binding fabric, make 3" wide continuous bias binding.

Fold the binding in half lengthwise, wrong sides together. Then attach it to the quilt front in a seam that penetrates all the layers. Turn the binding to the back and whipstitch it in place.

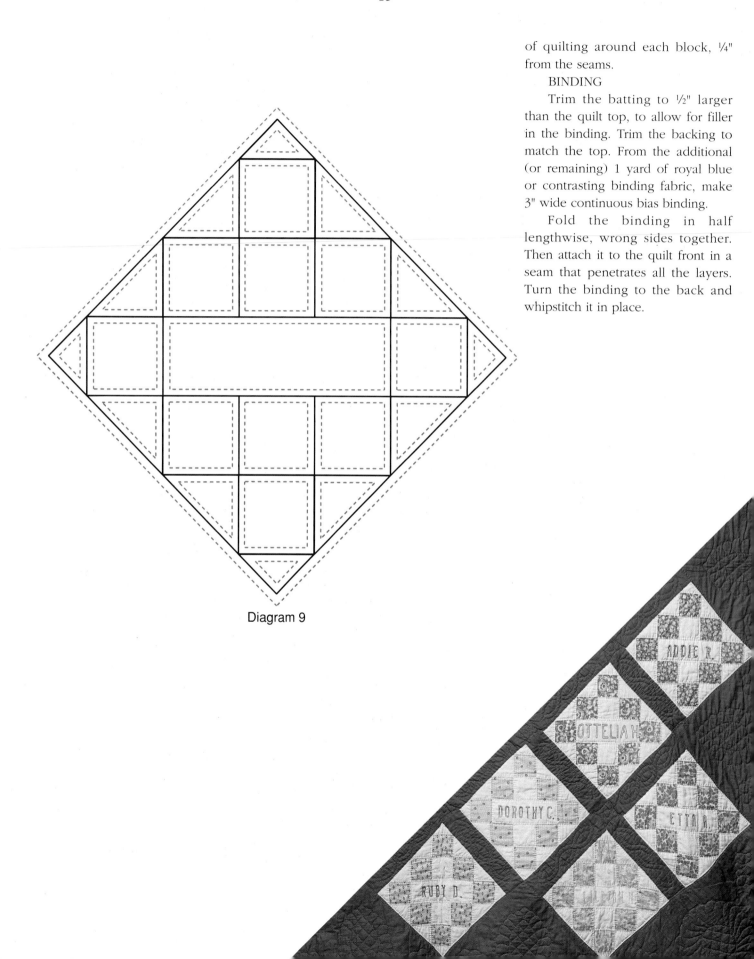

Diagram 9

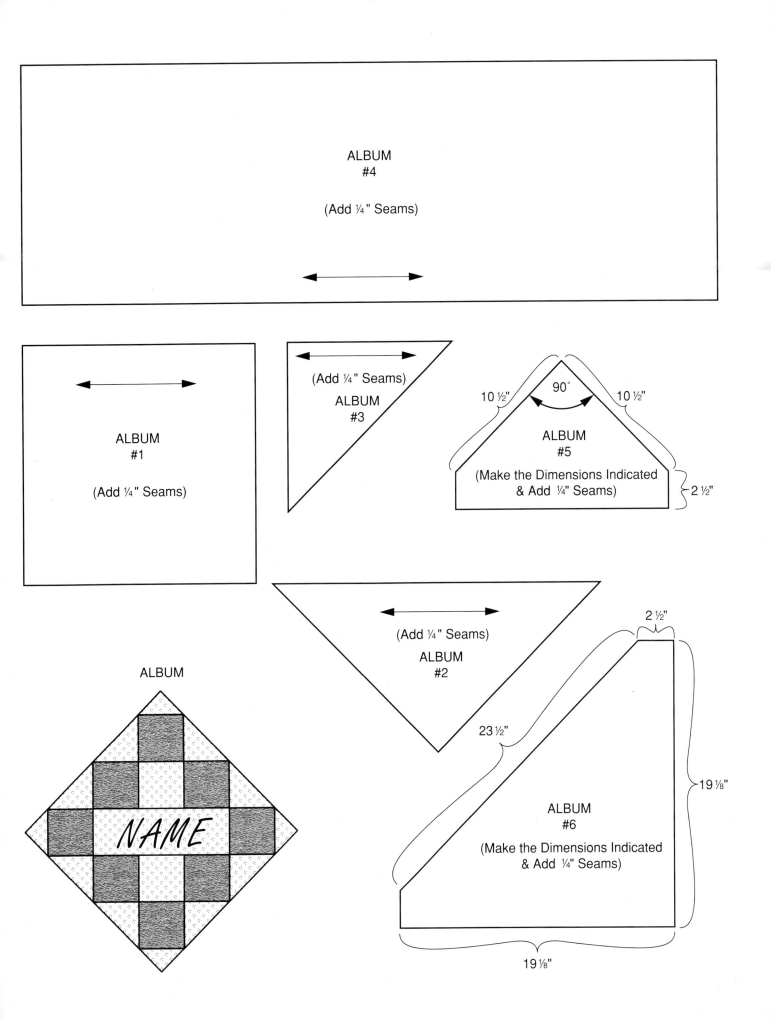

ALBUM
#4

(Add ¼" Seams)

ALBUM
#1

(Add ¼" Seams)

(Add ¼" Seams)
ALBUM
#3

90°
10 ½"   10 ½"
ALBUM
#5

(Make the Dimensions Indicated
& Add ¼" Seams)

2 ½"

(Add ¼" Seams)
ALBUM
#2

ALBUM

NAME

2 ½"

23 ½"

19 ⅛"

ALBUM
#6

(Make the Dimensions Indicated
& Add ¼" Seams)

19 ⅛"

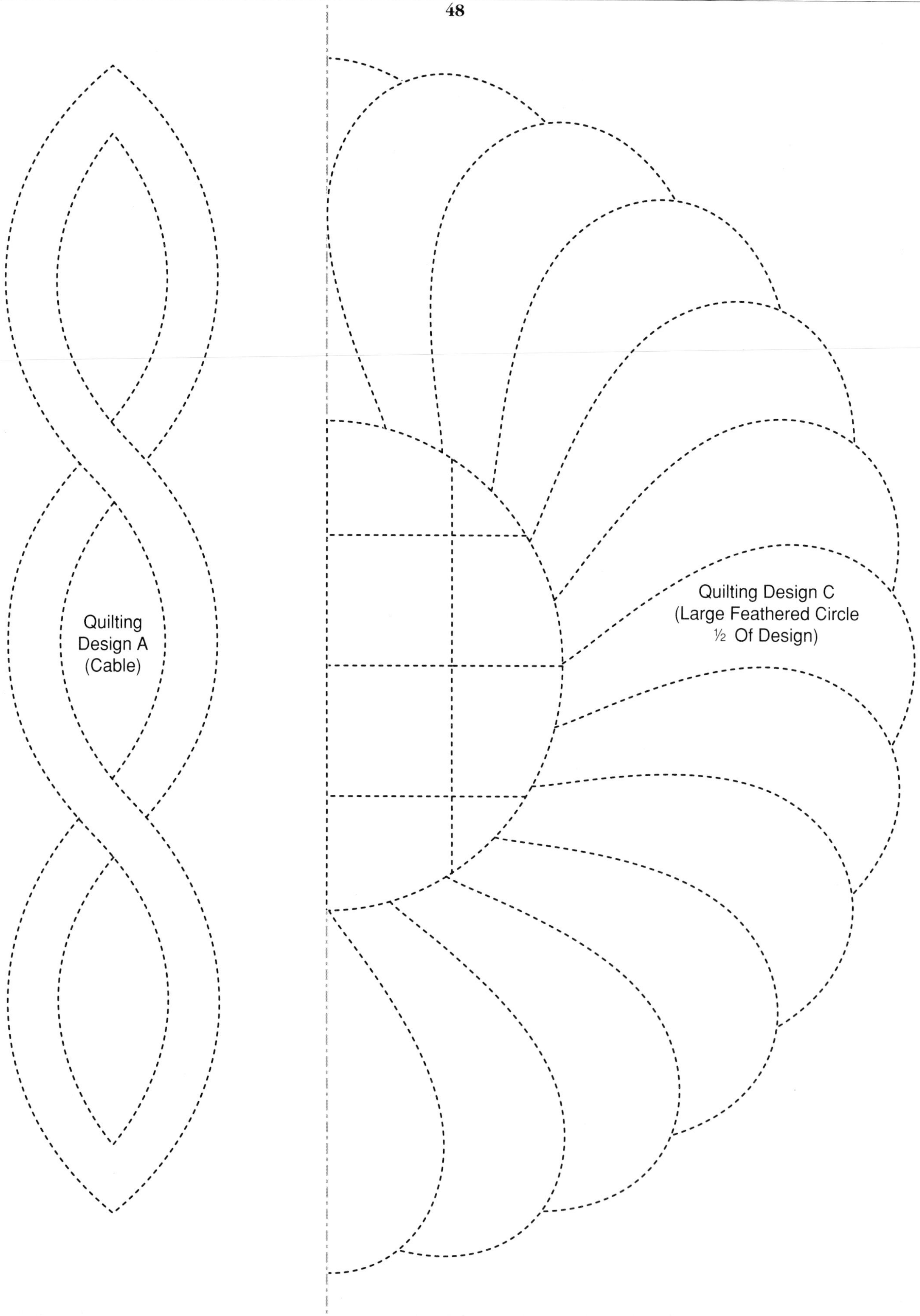

Quilting
Design A
(Cable)

Quilting Design C
(Large Feathered Circle
½ Of Design)

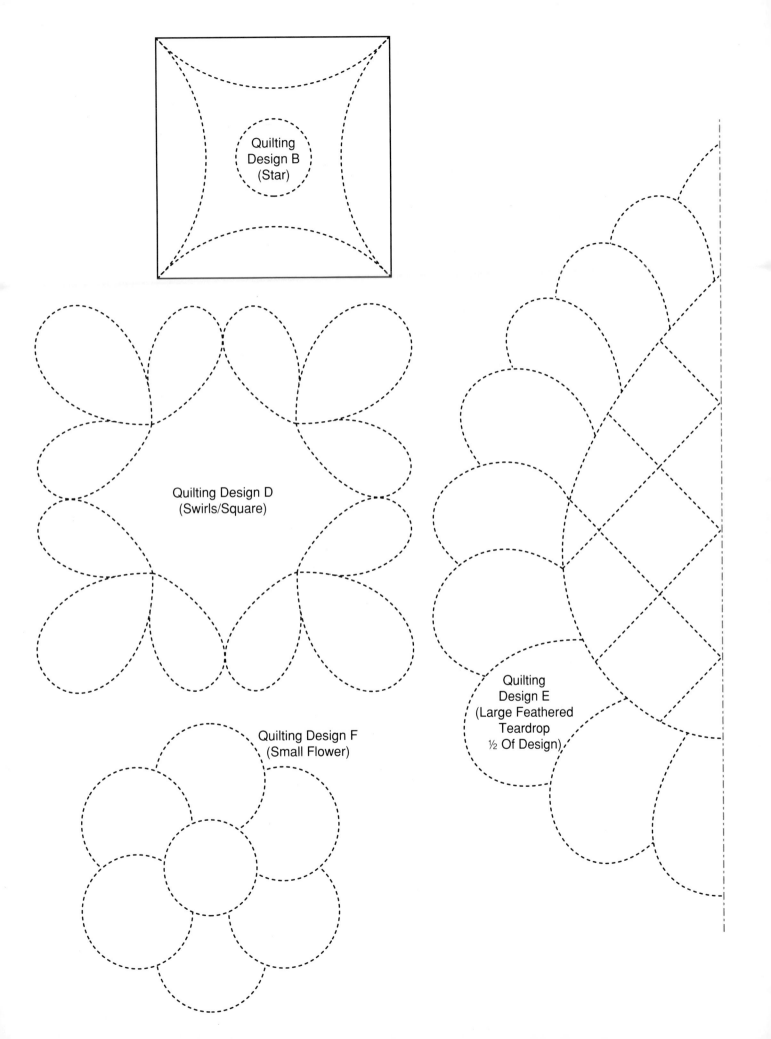

Quilting
Design B
(Star)

Quilting Design D
(Swirls/Square)

Quilting Design F
(Small Flower)

Quilting
Design E
(Large Feathered
Teardrop
½ Of Design)

ESSENTIAL INGREDIENTS
(IMPROVED NINE-PATCH)
QUILT BY DOROTHY GILBERTSON, ANN OHL, PAT SIMONSEN, AND THE AUTHOR
From the collection of Dorothy Gilbertson, Eau Claire, Wisconsin.

ESSENTIAL INGREDIENTS

Tuesday is a special day of the week for me. For nearly ten years I have been doing quilt-related things with a bevy of close friends nearly every Tuesday morning of the year. Meeting in the privacy of our homes, "quilting" commences at nine-thirty and finishes around noon, sometimes later if the project or topic of discussion demands.

Our Tuesday Quilters is not a large group. Our composition has changed over the years, but has never been more than the number that fits comfortably around our dining room tables, around a quilt frame, or into one vehicle for an excursion to a quilt show or shop.

Quilt projects are our reason for coming together. Other concerns – personal, family, community – are the reason we have remained together. In addition to being supported and strengthened in our quilting endeavors, we have nurtured each other personally and emotionally. Deep and warm friendships have been cultivated. An assemblage of women interested in quilts has evolved into a group of intimate friends.

About three years ago someone suggested that we make a friendship quilt. We all agreed it was an excellent idea. Although each of us had participated in other friendship projects over the years, we had overlooked the one group where a friendship quilt would be considered most appropriate. The notion of a quilt as an affirmation of our friendship was long overdue.

Soon we were discussing pattern and fabric ideas. Scraps seemed to be the consensus. A simple pattern, not too intricate, sounded attractive, as we were all working on other quilting projects. Bow Tie was the choice – very few templates, easy piecing, and not too time-consuming.

We probed deep into our scrap bags and shelves of fabric. No restrictions on colors and prints were made. The result was a colorful and cheerful blend that speaks to the personalities of all members of the group. Our Bow Tie friendship quilt is featured in the book *Award-Winning Scrap Quilts*.

That first Tuesday friendship quilt has come into my personal possession. Upon completion of the quilt, we had a drawing of names and I was the lucky winner. I was pleased and honored to be the recipient. I find great pleasure in using and showing the Bow Tie quilt. I find even greater pleasure in the recollection of happy moments in its making, of the sharing among the women. By any measure, our Bow Tie friendship quilt was a success.

Within a few weeks, discussion about a second friendship quilt could be heard. Little time was lost. Pattern and fabric ideas drifted around the room. Books and magazines were perused for inspiration. Having just completed a quilt with over three hundred and fifty print fabrics, the inclination now was toward solid fabrics. An uncomplicated pattern was the preference. An Improved Nine-Patch pattern in an Amish-style rendition caught our attention.

Soon we were back into our scrap bags and shelves of fabric, this time for solids in an unrestricted array of brightness and color. We cut and pieced the blocks. We paired triangles. We arranged fabrics into an overall design. And then we settled into a second winter of quilting around a frame – stitching, talking, sharing, sipping coffee, and sometimes staying for soup or brown bag lunch. We stitched a myriad of quilt designs and we also solved a myriad of problems – little everyday ones, medium-sized family ones, and huge world ones.

In her book *The Friendship Quilt Book*, author Mary Golden writes that "the friendship quilt survives because the need for quilts and the need for friendship survives. Warmth and love nourish our bodies and souls. These are essential ingredients of everyday life." For sure, they are essential ingredients on Tuesday mornings in Eau Claire, Wisconsin.

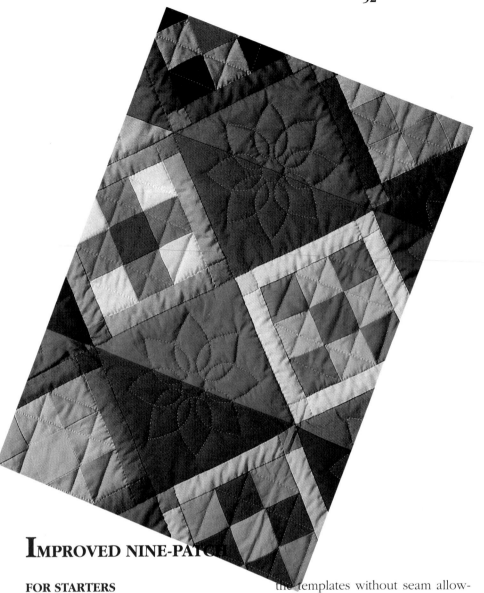

IMPROVED NINE-PATCH

FOR STARTERS

The following list will help you enjoy a smooth start and steady progress in your work on the Improved Nine-Patch Quilt. It contains a variety of general information about making the quilt:

- Wash and press all fabrics before you begin.
- A mixture of solid color fabrics (or scraps) can be used – as few as 5 or more than 150.
- All seams are ¼".
- For templates (patterns of the quilt pieces) use sturdy plastic, cardboard, or sandpaper, and be sure to note grain lines.
- Piecing may be done by hand or machine. For hand-piecing, make the templates without seam allowances, and add them when marking and cutting the fabrics. For machine-piecing, include the ¼" seam allowances on the templates.

- Thirty (30) pieced blocks are required.
- Twenty (20) paired triangle blocks are needed.
- Each block measures 8" x 8", finished.
- The narrow border is navy blue. The wide border is "country" blue.
- The finished size for the Improved Nine-Patch Quilt is 79" x 90½".

SUPPLIES

Use 44"/45" wide cotton or cotton/ polyester blend fabrics.

Quilt Top:

Solids: A variety of light, medium, and dark solid fabrics to total about 8 yards. If using new fabric, buy pieces ¼ yard or larger. If using scraps, the minimum size needed is about a 5" square for small pieced areas and a 10" square for the large paired triangles. The more variety and range of colors, the better.

Navy Blue: 3¼ yards (for the narrow borders and binding)

Medium ("country") Blue: 2¾ yards (for the wide borders)

Backing: you will need 5½ yards of good quality unbleached muslin

Batting: Use an 81" x 96" (double-size) bonded polyester batt

OTHER SUPPLIES

- Iron
- Material for templates
- Marking pencils or soap chips
- Scissors (for paper or fabric)
- Rulers
- Thread for piecing
- Pins
- Thread or safety pins for basting
- Quilting needles
- 2 spools natural color quilting thread
- Thimble
- Long straightedge
- Hoop or frame for quilting

READY TO WORK

COLOR KEY

The five fabrics used in the pieced blocks are coded A, B, C, D, and E. These may be your choice of a mixture of any light, medium, and dark solids. The paired triangle blocks are made from medium and dark solids which are coded M/D for Medium/Dark. Navy (N) and "country" blue (CB) are used for the quilt's borders.

TEMPLATES

Pattern pieces are numbered 1

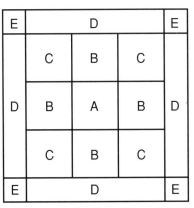

Diagram 1

through 5. Begin by making cardboard or plastic templates of all five shapes. Mark the grain line on each template. Quarter inch seams must also be added to all pieces.

CUTTING

Begin by grouping your fabrics into batches of 5 compatible colors. Use a mixture of lights, mediums and darks. Be sure there is some light/dark contrast between fabrics. Think of the group of 5 fabrics as being "in agreement" with each other, but not necessarily "coordinated."

Five fabrics are needed for each pieced block. For 30 blocks you could use as many as 150 colors. If you are working with fewer fabrics, you will have repeated fabrics throughout. If you are working with a large fabric mixture, it is probably easiest to cut all the pieces for one block at a time.

Begin with your first 5 fabrics. Designate the fabrics as A through E, according to Diagram 1, and cut the following pieces (a total of 17 pieces are required for each block):

Fabric A: Cut 1 of Template 1
Fabric B: Cut 4 of Template 1
Fabric C: Cut 4 of Template 1
Fabric D: Cut 4 of Template 2
Fabric E: Cut 4 of Template 3

Place the pieces right side up on a flat surface to be sure you have the correct shapes and numbers. Check for adequate contrast between adjacent fabrics.

Similarly, mark and cut fabrics for the remaining 29 blocks. If you are using only 5 fabrics or a small fabric mixture throughout the quilt, it will be easier for you to cut several pieces from one fabric before moving on to the the next fabric. If you use the same 5 fabrics in each block, cut the following:

Fabric A: Cut 30 of Template 1
Fabric B: Cut 120 of Template 1

Fabric C: Cut 120 of Template 1
Fabric D: Cut 120 of Template 2
Fabric E: Cut 120 of Template 3.

Next, cut the large triangles from the fabrics designated Medium and Dark (M/D). From a variety of colors, cut a total of 58 from Template 4. Then cut a total of 4 in mixed colors from Template 5.

BORDERS

From the Navy Blue (N) fabric, cut the following narrow borders (¼" seams included):

Cut 2 side borders 3¼" x 68½"
Cut 2 end borders 3¼" x 62½"

From the "country" blue (CB) fabric, cut the following wider borders (¼" seams included):

Cut 2 side borders 9" x 74"
Cut 2 end borders 9" x 79½"

PUTTING IT TOGETHER

BLOCK PIECING

Refer to Diagram 2 for a graphic illustration of the pieced block. Collect the 17 pieces needed to complete one block (as shown in Diagram 1). Place the pieces right side up on a flat surface according to the diagram. Piece according to these steps.

• Piece C squares on opposite sides of a B square, as indicated by the arrows in Diagram 3. Make 2 of these units. Press seams toward the center.

• Stitch B squares on opposite sides of an A square, as in Diagram 4. Press seams away from the center.

• Join the three units in a nine-patch fashion, with horizontal seams as shown in Diagram 5. Be careful to "butterfly" the seams at each junction. This will occur naturally if the seams have been pressed as suggested above. Press seams away from the center.

• Stitch D rectangles on opposite sides of the nine-patch unit as shown in Diagram 6. Press seams

Diagram 2

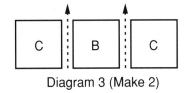

Diagram 3 (Make 2)

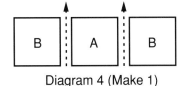

Diagram 4 (Make 1)

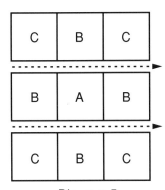

Diagram 5

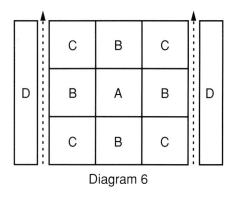

Diagram 6

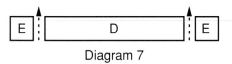

Diagram 7

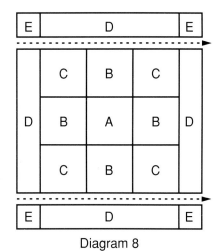

Diagram 8

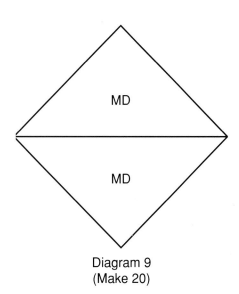

Diagram 9
(Make 20)

toward the outside.

•Stitch E squares on the opposite ends of a D rectangle, as shown in Diagram 7. Press seams toward the rectangle. Make 2 of these units.

•To complete the block, sew E-D-E units on the top and bottom of the center nine-patch, as shown in Diagram 8. Press seams toward the outside.

•Complete the other 29 pieced blocks in a similar fashion.

PAIRED TRIANGLES

Refer to Diagram 9. Stitch two Medium/Dark (M/D) large triangles (different colors) to form a block. Make 20 of these blocks with mixed colors. Press seams to one side.

ASSEMBLY

Refer to Diagram 10 for a general layout of the quilt top. Collect the 30 pieced blocks, 20 paired triangle blocks, 18 (M/D) large triangles, and 4 corner triangles. Lay the blocks on a large flat surface (floor, bed, or wall) and arrange them in a pleasing design. Note the color placement and contrasts of light and dark fabrics. When you have settled on a design arrangement, you are ready to assemble the top.

The quilt top is assembled in smaller units designated I, II, III, IV, and V, as shown in Diagram 11. The arrows indicate the directions to press the seams.

Diagram 10

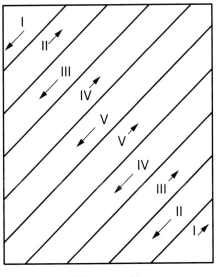

Diagram 11

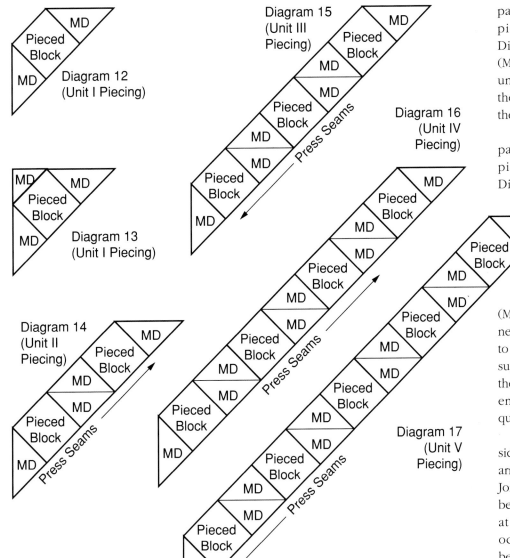

Diagram 12
(Unit I Piecing)

Diagram 13
(Unit I Piecing)

Diagram 14
(Unit II Piecing)

Diagram 15
(Unit III Piecing)

Diagram 16
(Unit IV Piecing)

Diagram 17
(Unit V Piecing)

• To assemble Unit I for the upper left corner of the quilt, stitch large Medium/Dark (M/D) triangles on opposite sides of a pieced block, as shown in Diagram 12. Add the small corner triangle (M/D) to complete Unit I as shown in Diagram 13. Press the seams to one side, as suggested by the arrows. Make a similar unit for the opposite corner of the quilt.

• To assemble Unit II, stitch a paired triangle block (M/D) between two pieced blocks, as shown in Diagram 14. Add a large triangle (M/D) to each end, to complete the unit. Press seams as suggested by the arrow. Make a similar unit for the opposite corner of the quilt.

• To assemble Unit III, stitch 2 paired triangle blocks between 3 pieced blocks, according to Diagram 15. Add a large triangle (M/D) to each end to complete the unit. Press seams as suggested by the arrow. Make a similar unit for the other corner of the quilt.

• To assemble Unit IV, stitch 3 paired triangle blocks between 4 pieced blocks, according to Diagram 16. Add a large triangle (M/D) to each end to complete the unit. Press seams as suggested by the arrow. Make a similar unit for the other side of the quilt.

• To assemble Unit V, stitch 4 paired triangle blocks between 5 pieced blocks, according to Diagram 17. Add a large triangle (M/D) to one end and a small corner triangle (M/D) to the other end to complete the unit. Press seams as suggested. Make a similar unit (with the corner triangle on the opposite end) for the other section of the quilt.

Lay the 10 pieced units right sides up according to the diagonal arrangement shown in Diagram 11. Join the sections in diagonal seams, being careful to butterfly the seams at each intersection. This should occur naturally if the units have been pressed as suggested.

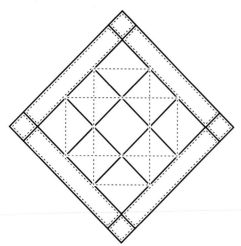

Diagram 18

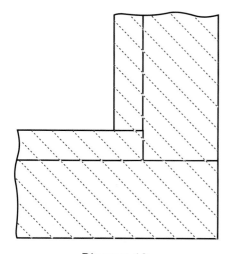

Diagram 19

BORDERS

Add the narrow Navy Blue (N) borders first. Stitch the side borders to the assembled center, referring back to Diagram 10. Then add the end borders.

Next, add the wide Country Blue (CB) borders. Add the sides first, then the ends, to complete the quilt top.

THE FINISHING TOUCH

QUILTING

From the 5½ yards of unbleached muslin, cut two 2¾ yard lengths. Keep one intact (about 42" wide). From the other piece, cut two 21" widths. Join a 21" width to each side of the intact center panel. Press the seams toward the outside.

Place the quilt backing right side down on a large flat surface. Smooth the batting over it. Place the pressed quilt top over the batting, right side up. Pin or thread baste the three layers together for quilting.

Make stencils of the three quilting designs:

Design A (full flower)
Design B (half flower)

Design C (one quarter flower)

Mark and quilt a full flower in the center of each paired triangle block. Mark and quilt a half flower on each of the 18 outer (M/D) triangles. Mark and quilt a quarter flower on each of the 4 corner triangles. Use natural color quilting thread.

Refer to Diagram 18 for suggested quilting on the pieced blocks: two rectangles in the center nine-patch, one superimposed over the other, and "in-the-ditch" quilting in the outer rectangle/square areas.

Suggested border quilting is illustrated in Diagram 19: Diagonal parallel lines that cross both the narrow and wide borders.

BINDING

Trim the batting to ½" larger than the quilt top, to allow for filler in the binding. Trim the backing to match the top. From the remaining Navy Blue (N) fabric, make 3" wide continuous bias binding.

Fold the binding in half, wrong sides together. Then attach it to the quilt front in a seam that penetrates all the layers. Turn the binding to the back and whipstitch it in place.

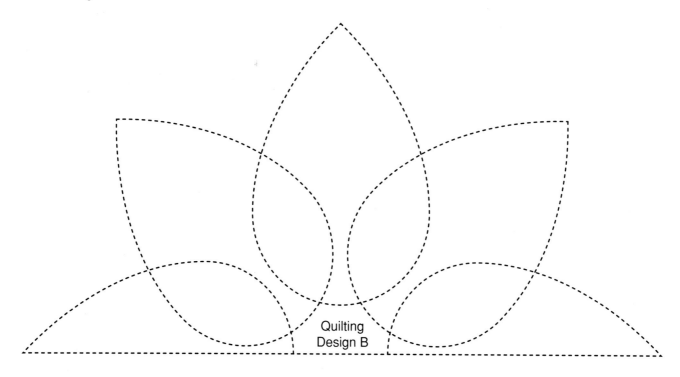

Quilting
Design B

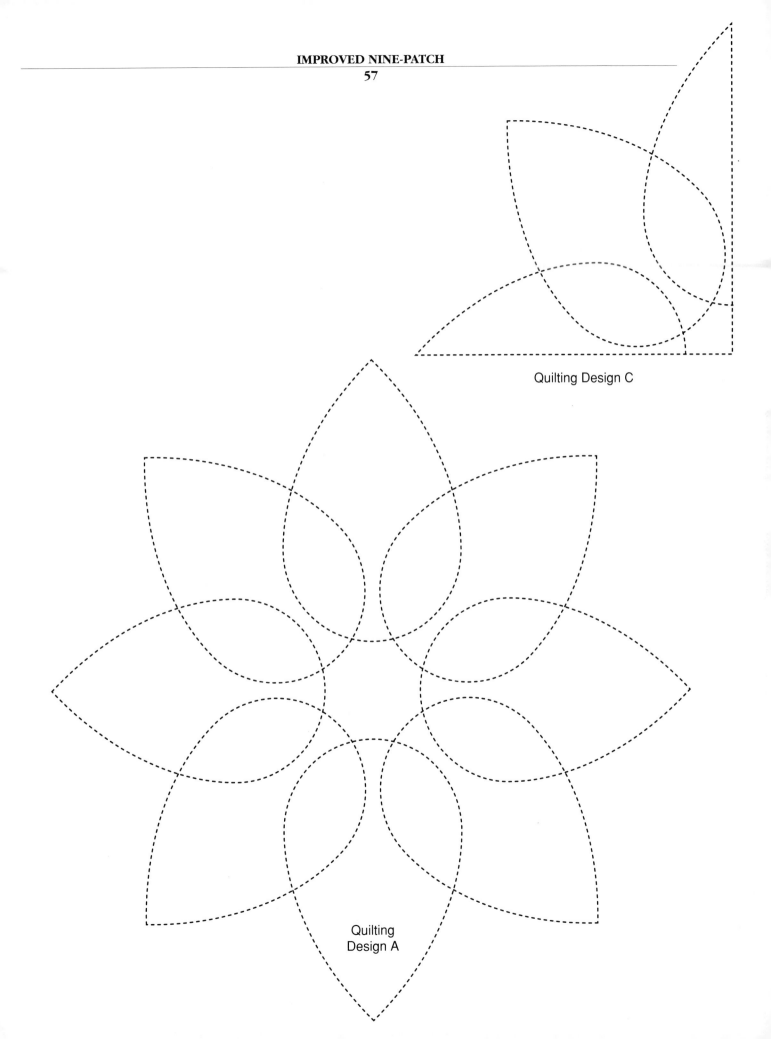

Quilting Design C

Quilting
Design A

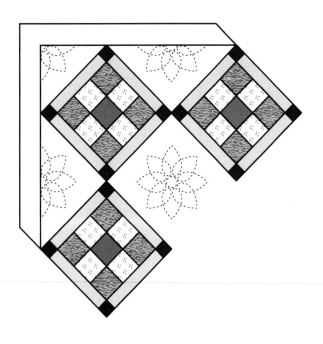

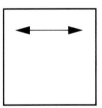

IMPROVED 9-PATCH
#1

(Add ¼" Seams)

IMPROVED 9-PATCH
#3
(Add ¼" Seams)

IMPROVED 9-PATCH
#2

(Add ¼" Seams)

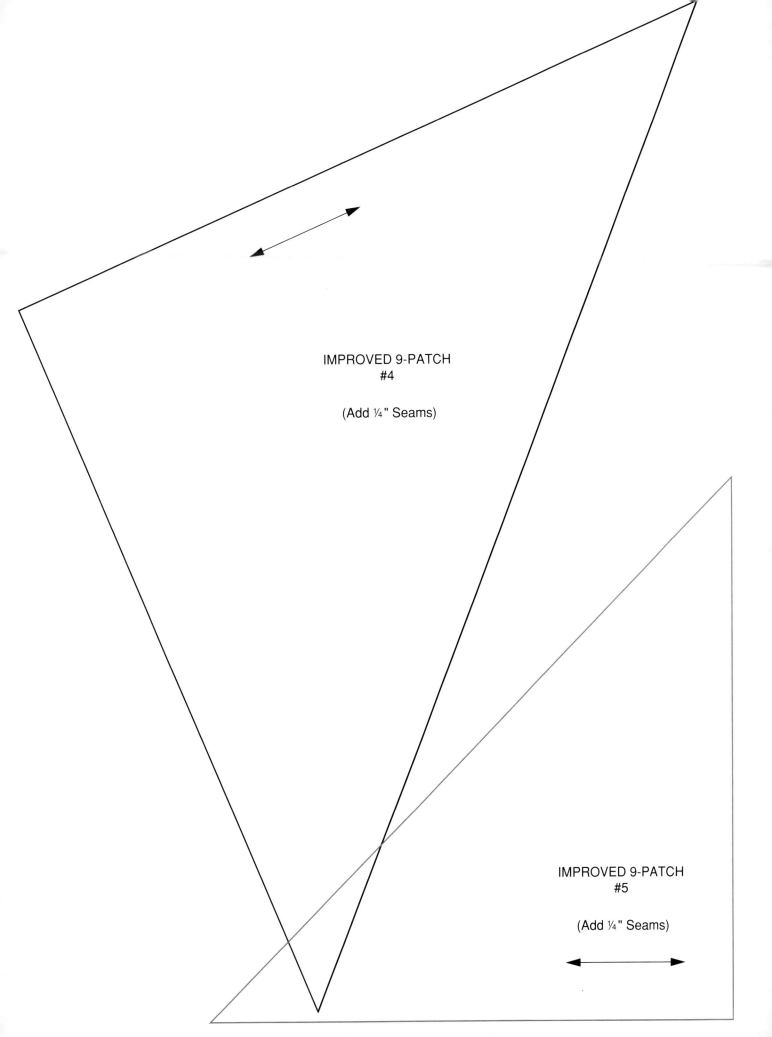

IMPROVED 9-PATCH
#4

(Add ¼" Seams)

IMPROVED 9-PATCH
#5

(Add ¼" Seams)

ONE THOUSAND NINE HUNDRED AND TWENTY FABRICS
(OCEAN WAVES)
QUILT BY KATHY BARTEL, DOROTHY GILBERTSON, MAGGIE GUSTAFSON,
ANN OHL, PAT SIMONSEN, AND THE AUTHOR.
From The Collection Of Kathy Bartel, Eau Claire, Wisconsin.

ONE THOUSAND NINE HUNDRED AND TWENTY FABRICS

Making a charm quilt is an ambitious undertaking. So when I embarked on a charm quilt project, I did it with the cooperation of five close quilting friends whose resources and energy could be combined in one friendly endeavor.

Our "Ocean Waves Charm Quilt," complete with its one thousand nine hundred and twenty little triangles, each cut from a different fabric, is the result. We call it our 1920 quilt.

By definition, a "charm" quilt has no two pieces cut from the same fabric. Many charm quilts are pure collections of pieces from many different fabrics and scraps, each cut in the same shape, assembled in one fascinating composition. Some charm quilts are planned for their design effect, with careful thought given to pattern choice and color arrangements. Our friendship group selected the Ocean Waves pattern, a natural charm choice with its multitude of repeated same-size triangles.

We dug into our fabric accumulations and began cutting triangles. By our fourth meeting, after we had each dug fairly deep, we still needed 250 additional fabrics. We simply had no idea of the magnitude of fabrics needed to reach the number 1,920. We continued our search into drawers and closets, looking deeper and discovering older fabrics from our mothers' and grandmothers' scraps. More triangles were cut, and duplicates were spotted and eliminated along the way. We began the pleasurable task of arranging the blocks. Our group did this on my living room floor. Blocks were layed out in rows and columns, then arranged and re-arranged until the group members were satisfied with the composition.

We took the pieced top to the local fabric center for selection of the border fabrics. With the 1,920-piece top and bolts of fabric strewn across counter tops, personal preferences were expressed and decisions made.

Weekly quilting sessions were scheduled, and the five friends and I slowly and steadily stitched across the array of fabrics. Comments regarding fabrics were frequent ("Oh, I remember this one!" "They don't make fabric like this anymore." "Who would think of putting this in a quilt?" "Isn't this about the prettiest/cutest/homeliest fabric you ever saw?). Each section of quilting was like stitching on a new project because nothing was ever the same. And one long Wisconsin winter was made more tolerable with the sessions spent stitching on and admiring the fabrics.

My friends and I have a custom of drawing names for our friendship quilts. Eligible names are tossed in a hat, and one is pulled out. Our Ocean Waves quilt has found a happy home. It's owner, Kathy Bartel, reports that it fits her queen-size bed perfectly, and coordinates nicely with the carpet and draperies, too.

My friends and I are ready to begin planning our next quilt. Those whose names are still in the hat are especially eager to get started.

Ocean Waves

FOR STARTERS

The following list will help you enjoy a smooth start and steady progress in your work on the Ocean Waves quilt.

- Wash and press all fabrics before you begin.
- To make an authentic "charm" quilt, no two fabrics are repeated, so a total of 1,920 different fabric triangles are required.
- A reasonable alternative is to use randomly repeated scrap fabrics throughout the quilt.
- All seams are ¼".
- For templates (patterns of the quilt pieces) use sturdy plastic, cardboard, or sandpaper, and be sure to note grain lines.
- Piecing may be done by hand or machine. For hand-piecing, make the templates without seam allowances, and add them when marking and cutting the fabrics. For machine-piecing, include the ¼" seam allowances on the templates.
- Each pieced block measures 8" x 8", finished.
- Eighty (80) pieced blocks are needed.
- The inner border is 2" wide; the outer border 6", finished.
- The finished size for the Ocean Waves charm quilt is 80" x 96".

SUPPLIES:

Use 44"/45" cotton or cotton/ polyester blend fabrics.

Quilt Top:

Scraps: A large variety of mixed light and dark scraps (anything goes), for a total of 1,920 (that's one thousand nine hundred twenty) for a true charm quilt. The minimum scrap is about 3" square. Medium Blue (for background): 1¾ yards

Dark Blue Solid (for inner border and binding): 2½ yards

Dark Blue Print (for outer border): 3 yards

Backing: 6 yards of good quality unbleached muslin

Batting: Use an 81" x 96" (double-size) bonded polyester batt

OTHER SUPPLIES

- Iron
- Material for templates
- Marking pencils or soap chips
- Scissors (for paper and fabric)
- Rulers
- Thread for piecing
- Pins
- Thread or safety pins for basting
- Quilting needles
- 3 spools natural color quilting thread
- Thimble
- Long straightedge or masking tape
- Hoop or frame for quilting

READY TO WORK

COLOR KEY
L=Light Scrap
D= Dark Scrap
MB= Medium Blue Solid
DB= Dark Blue Solid
P= Dark Blue Print

TEMPLATES

Begin by making templates of the two Ocean Wave triangle pieces (#1 and #2). Mark the grain lines and note that ¼" seams must be added to all sides on each piece.

CUTTING

Begin with your scrap fabric. Cut a small triangle, (Template 1) for each fabric. Adhere to the suggested grain lines whenever possible. Cut a total of 1,920 triangles. Twenty-four (24) triangles (12 light and 12 dark) are needed for each 8" block.

Continue with the Medium Blue (MB) fabric and cut 160 large triangles (Template 2).

From the Dark Blue Solid (DB) fabric, cut the following pieces for the inner borders (allowances for seams and mitering included):

Cut 2 side borders 2½" x 84½"
Cut 2 end borders 2½" x 68½"

From the Dark Blue Print (P) fabric, cut the following outer border pieces (allowances for seams and mitering included):

Cut 2 side borders 6½" x 96½"
Cut 2 end borders 6½" x 80½"

PUTTING IT TOGETHER

BLOCK PIECING

Refer to Diagram 1 and 2 for illustrations of the Ocean Wave block. Collect the 24 small triangles (half light and half dark) needed for one block. Join a light triangle to a dark triangle to form a square, as in Diagram 3. Complete 10 squares.

Arrange the 10 pieced squares and the remaining 4 triangles to complete the unit as shown in Diagram 4.

Attach the two Medium Blue (MB) corner triangles to complete the 8" (finished) block.

Press all seams to one side, in a uniform manner.

Make 3 more 8" blocks. Then join these 4 blocks together to form the 16" units as illustrated in

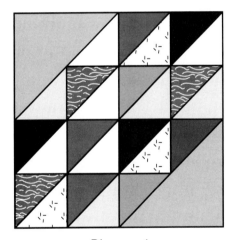

Diagram 1

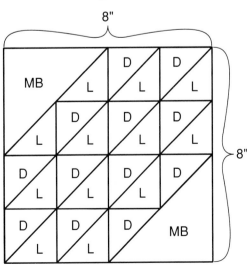

Diagram 2

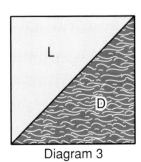

Diagram 3

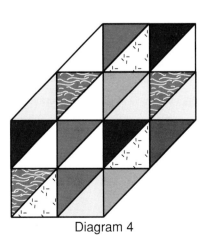

Diagram 4

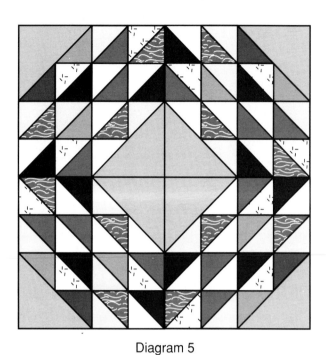

Diagram 5

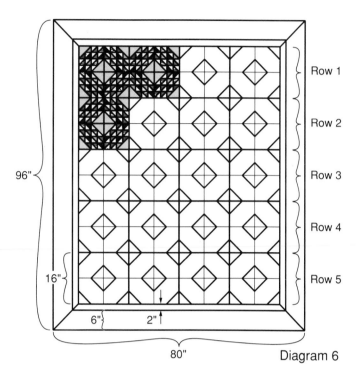

Row 1

Row 2

Row 3

Row 4

Row 5

96"

16"

6"

2"

80"

Diagram 6

Diagram 5.

You will need twenty (20) 16" blocks for the full-size quilt top.

ASSEMBLY

Refer to Diagram 6 for the quilt layout. The 16" blocks are arranged in 4 columns and 5 rows. Lay the units on a large flat surface and experiment with placement to find a satisfactory color arrangement. Then piece Row 1 in short vertical seams, according to Diagram 7. Join Rows 2 through 5 in a similar fashion. Join the 5 rows in longer horizontal seams to complete the center of the quilt.

BORDERS

To complete the quilt top, attach the Dark Blue Solid (DB) inner 2" borders. Miter the corners. Finally, add the Dark Blue Print (P) outer 6" borders. Miter the corners.

QUILTING

From the 6 yards of muslin backing fabric, cut two 3-yard lengths. Keep one intact (about 42" wide). From the other piece, cut two 21" widths. Join a 21" width to each side of the intact center panel. Press the seams toward the outside.

Place the quilt backing right side down on a large flat surface. Smooth the batting over it. Place the pressed quilt top over the batting, right side up. Pin or thread baste the three layers together for quilting.

Using a long straightedge and a washable fabric marker or soap chip, mark the diagonal quilting lines as suggested in Diagram 8, page 65. Quilt, using natural color quilting thread.

On the narrow inner border, quilt along each edge, about ½" from the seam.

On the outer border, mark and quilt the zigzag design shown in Diagram 9, page 66.

BINDING

Trim the batting to ½" larger than the quilt top, to allow for filler in the binding. Trim the backing to match the top. From the remaining Dark Blue (DB) fabric, make 3" wide continuous bias binding.

Fold the binding in half lengthwise, wrong sides together. Then attach it to the quilt front in a seam that penetrates all the layers. Turn the binding to the back and whipstitch it in place.

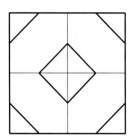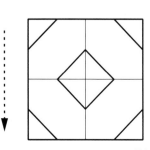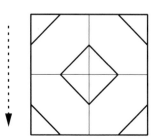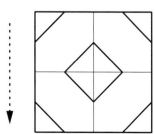

Diagram 7

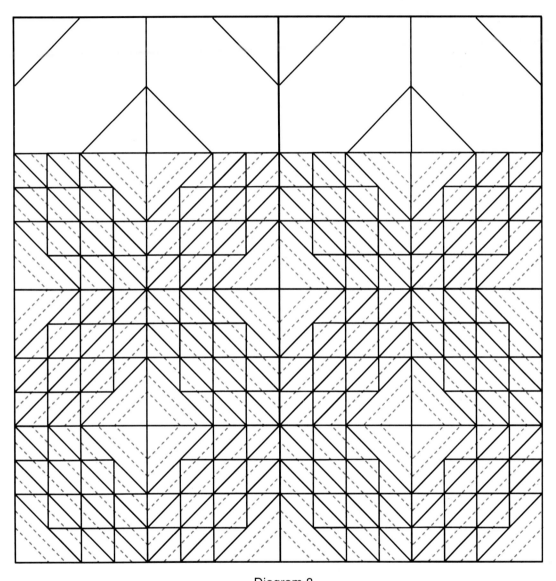

Diagram 8

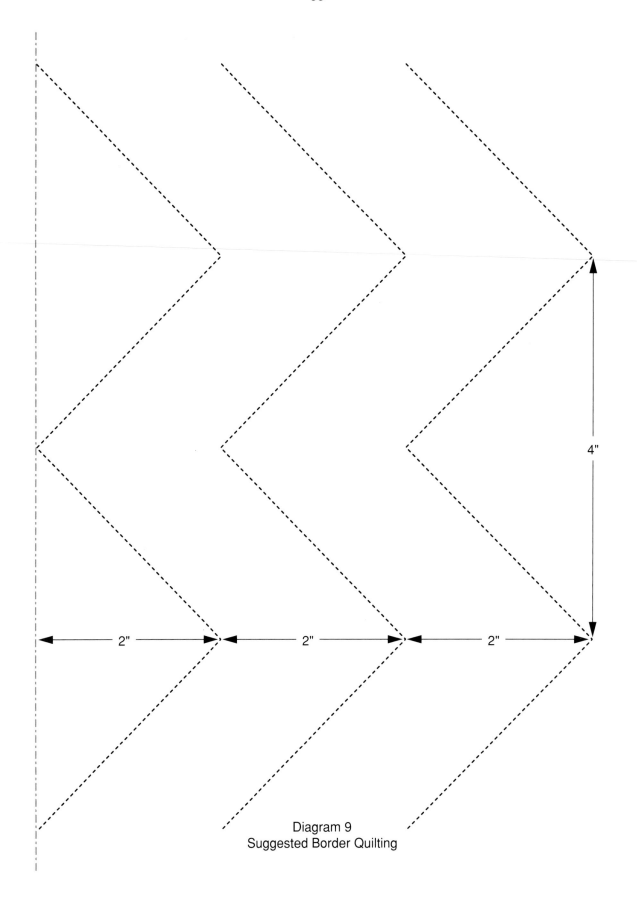

Diagram 9
Suggested Border Quilting

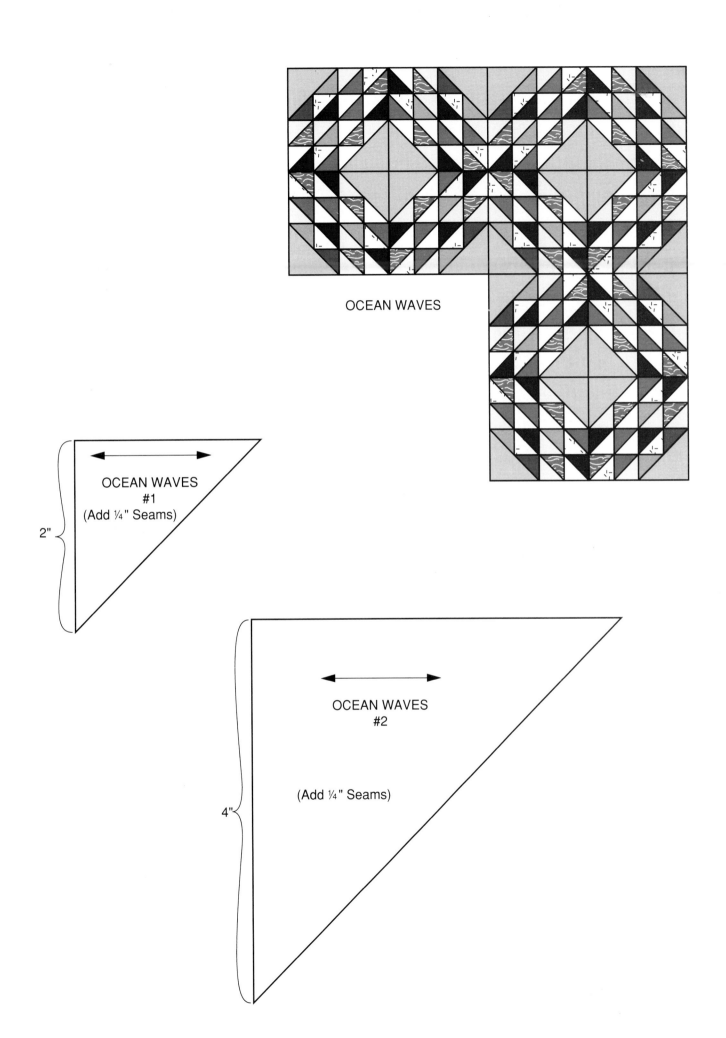

OCEAN WAVES

OCEAN WAVES
#1
(Add ¼" Seams)

2"

OCEAN WAVES
#2

(Add ¼" Seams)

4"

PICKING UP WHERE GRANDMOTHER LEFT OFF
(SUNBONNET SUE)
QUILT BY THE AUTHOR

PICKING UP WHERE GRANDMOTHER LEFT OFF

The discussion about Sunbonnet Sue continues. Is she really the darling of the twentieth century American quilter, or is she the lowest common denominator of quilt patterns? My mind was made up before the discussion became serious.

My grandmother, Louise Hass Steinbach, had a Sunbonnet Sue quilt in progress at the time of her death in 1963. That was about ten years before I became interested in quilting. When I did get started, my mother gave me my grandmother's box of scraps and the "in-progress" applique and piecing that she had saved. Sunbonnet Sue was among her unfinished projects.

A few bonnets and dresses had been cut. Two Sunbonnet Sues had been carefully appliqued and embroidered onto muslin sugar sacks. Grandma's original brown paper pattern pieces were still intact, waiting for a willing quilter to pick up where she had left off.

When I began working on her Sunbonnet Sue quilt, I was in an early stage of quilt design. My previous quilts has been strictly traditional – a Dresden plate, an Eight-Point Star, a Double Wedding Ring, and a Grandmother's Flower Garden. Sunbonnet Sue was an appropriate quilt on which to hone my elementary applique skills.

The first pleasurable task was to inventory the pieces Grandma had already cut. She had bonnets and dresses, hands, arms, and feet for ten girls. I wanted to make a bed-size quilt, so I decided to add to her array of fabrics. The result was a mixture of old and new, some fabrics that date from the 1940's and 1950's, some that were purchased new in the late 1970's. The fabrics cover a fifty year span of time. If you look carefully at the color photograph, you can probably detect the older prints – a pink and black plaid, a print with an "Eastern" flavor, green and peach geometrics, a delicate rosebud print, and a lavender floral spray. Newer fabrics appear in deeper and bolder colors of red, blue, and teal, the fabrics more familiar in feeling.

The twenty girls each wear a dress from a different fabric, with a coordinated bonnet in a solid color. Following the design suggested by my grandmother, I embroidered decorative stitches on the bonnets, hands, and feet. I chose a peach colored latticework, more in keeping with earlier quilts from my grandmother's time. Simple outline quilting and diagonal lines frame the blocks and help to set off each girl.

The ubiquitous Sunbonnet Sue has been subject to what some quilters view as contemporary abuse. Yes, one can tire of seeing yet another rendition of this faceless charming child. Strains of "Oh, please, no, not another Sunbonnet Sue quilt" have been heard. But she continues to make nationwide appearances in crib quilts, in sampler quilts, and even in cartoons. These familiar bonnetted figures have been the subject for both a serious comprehensive study by Dolores Hinson and a light-hearted cartoon series by Jean Ray Laury. Sunbonnet Sue fits the bill for both serious and comic.

A few years ago I hung the treasured Sunbonnet Sue blocks that my grandmother had embroidered onto sugar sacks in my quilting room. I invited a quilt friend who does her own creative quilting designs to the room to see a quilt I was working on, my latest pieced innovation on the quilt frame. It was a colorful design with intricate piecing and elaborate quilting, and I was in the midst of quilting it. My friend's eyes were drawn immediately to the Sunbonnet Sues on the wall. She exclaimed, "Why, Judy Florence, I never thought I would see a Sunbonnet Sue in your house!" Caught off guard, I wasn't sure just how to respond. I only knew I had an immediate and undeniable urge to defend my Sunbonnet girls, probably more because they were from my grandmother's hands than because they needed my meager protection.

The incident also confirmed that perhaps my inclination for quilting does have a genetic connection. Although my maternal grandmother did piecing, applique, and quilting for many of her seventy-three years, I did not learn quilting from her, or ever quilt with her. At the time of her death, I had just begun my college years, and quiltmaking was probably the farthest thing from my mind. But there was no denying the inclination ten years later. And the arrival of my grandmother's box of fabrics and mid-stream projects confirmed the genetic connection for me.

Grandma's scraps continue to appear in my quilt designs. Several are included in my Attic Windows and Virginal Reel quilts found elsewhere in this book. And I'll continue to use them, mainly as nostalgic reminders and affirmations of my family's quiltmaking past.

SUNBONNET SUE

FOR STARTERS

The following list will help you enjoy a smooth start and steady progress in your work on the Sunbonnet Sue quilt. It contains a variety of general information about making the quilt:

- Wash and press all fabrics before you begin.
- A mixture of fabric scraps in both prints and solids is a good choice for Sunbonnet Sue.
- For templates (patterns of the quilt pieces) use sturdy plastic, cardboard, or sandpaper, and be sure to note grain lines.
- The Sunbonnet Sue quilt requires hand applique. Use the applique method of your choice.
- Scant ¼" seams are recommended for applique pieces.
- Use ¼" seams for piecing the lattice strips and borders.
- Twenty (20) applique blocks are required.
- Each block measures 14" square, finished.
- Blocks are separated with 2½" wide lattice and borders, finished.
- The finished size for the Sunbonnet Sue quilt is 68½" x 85".

SUPPLIES

Use 44"/45" wide cotton or cotton/polyester blend fabrics.

Quilt Top:

Print Scraps: 20 different fabrics in a variety of colors, minimum scrap size about 8" x 8". For new fabric, buy ¼ yard of each fabric.

Solid Scraps: same as print scraps

White: 4½ yards for background and small squares

Peach: 2½ yards for lattice and borders

Binding: Buy an additional 1 yard of white solid fabric.

Backing: 5½ yards of solid white or other color of your choice to match fabrics in the quilt top.

Batting: Use a 72" x 90" (twin-size) bonded polyester batt.

OTHER SUPPLIES

- Iron
- Material for templates
- Marking pencils or soap chips
- Scissors (for paper and fabric)
- Rulers
- Thread for piecing
- Thread for applique in colors to match the scrap fabrics
- Pins
- Embroidery floss in mixed colors to match the solid scraps
- Thread or safety pins for basting
- Quilting needles
- 2 spools of white quilting thread
- Thimble
- Long straightedge
- Hoop or frame for quilting

READY TO WORK

FABRIC KEY:

P= Print

S= Solid

W= White

L= Lattice

B= Border

TEMPLATES

Begin by making templates of all six Sunbonnet Sue pattern pieces (#1, 2, 3, 4, 5, and 6). Mark the suggested grain lines on each template. Also mark the top of templates 1-5. Note that scant ¼" seam allowances must be added on all sides of each applique piece. Also add ¼" seams to the square.

CUTTING

Begin with the 20 Print (P) fabrics. From each fabric cut one dress piece (Template 1) and one arm piece (Template 2). You will need 20 dresses and 20 arm pieces.

Continue with the 20 Solid (S) fabrics. Cut a bonnet (Template 3), a hand (Template 4), and feet (Template 5) from each fabric.

Next, cut 20 background squares, each 14½" x 14½" (seam allowances included), from the White (W) fabric. Then cut 12 corner squares (Template 6).

Last, cut the following borders and lattice strips from the Peach colored fabric:

Cut 2 side borders 3" x 80½"
(allowances for seams included)
Cut 2 end borders 3" x 69"
(allowances for seams included)
Cut 31 lattice strips 3" x 14½"
(allowances for seams included)

PUTTING IT TOGETHER

APPLIQUE

Begin by locating the center of a white (W) background square. Do this by folding the square in half in both directions.

Collect the 5 pieces for one Sunbonnet Sue. Turn under the scant ¼" allowances on each piece. It is NOT necessary to turn under the top edge (the "V") of the dress, the flat end of the hand, or the top edge of the feet, as these will be tucked behind adjacent pieces. Press

or baste the turned edges.

Refer to Diagram 1 for placement of the applique pieces. Place the dress on the background square, centering it from side to side. Place the bonnet over the top edge of the dress and center the combined pieces from top to bottom. Pin in place.

Place an arm piece over the dress. Tuck a hand piece under the end of the arm. Place the feet piece beneath the dress and tuck it under the lower edge of the dress. Pin or baste all pieces.

Applique all pieces with small invisible stitches. Use thread in a color to match each fabric, changing thread color, if necessary.

Refer to the pattern pieces for suggested decorative stitching on the bonnet, arm, hand, and feet. Use embroidery thread in a color to complement the fabrics. Use decorative running stitches.

Make a total of 20 appliqued Sunbonnet Sues.

LATTICEWORK and BORDERS

Refer to Diagram 2 for the layout of the Sunbonnet Sue quilt. Make a latticework strip by piecing 4 lattice pieces (L) and 3 White (W) squares, as in Diagram 3. Make 4 of these lattice strips.

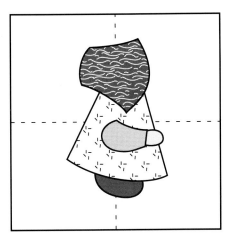

Diagram 1

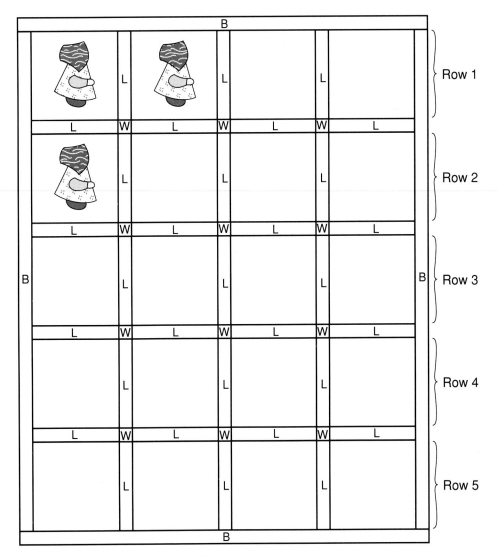

Diagram 2

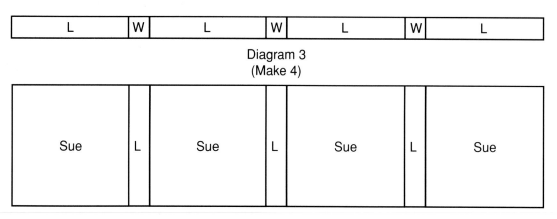

L	W	L	W	L	W	L

Diagram 3
(Make 4)

Sue	L	Sue	L	Sue	L	Sue

Diagram 4
(Make 5)

Arrange the 20 Sunbonnet Sues according to Diagram 2 (4 across, 5 down). Piece Row #1 by stitching 4 blocks and 3 lattice (L) pieces together, as in Diagram 4. Complete the other 4 rows.

Next, place a narrow pieced lattice strip between each row of appliqued blocks. Join together in longer horizontal cross seams.

To complete the quilt top, add the peach side borders, and then the end borders.

THE FINISHING TOUCH

QUILTING

From the 5½ yards of backing fabric, cut two, 2¾ yard lengths. Keep one intact (about 42" wide). From the other piece, cut two 21" widths. Join a 21" width to each side of the intact center panel. Press seams toward the outside.

Place the quilt backing right side down on a large flat surface. Smooth the batting over it. Place the pressed quilt top over the batting, right side up. Pin or thread baste the three layers together for quilting.

Use a washable marking pencil or soap chip to mark the quilting lines suggested in Diagram 5:

• Quilt ¼" from the edge of each block.

• Quilt diagonal corner "framing" lines on each block.

• Quilt around each Sunbonnet Sue, about ¼" away from the pieces.

• Quilt along the lattice pieces about ½" from each long edge.

• Quilt two lines ¼" and ½" from the inner edge of the 4 border pieces.

BINDING

Trim the batting to ½" larger than the quilt top, to allow for filler in the binding. Trim the backing to match the top. From the 1 yard of white binding fabric, make 3" wide continuous bias binding.

Fold the binding in half lengthwise, wrong sides together. Then attach it to the quilt front in a seam that penetrates all the layers. Turn the binding to the back and whipstitch it in place.

Diagram 5

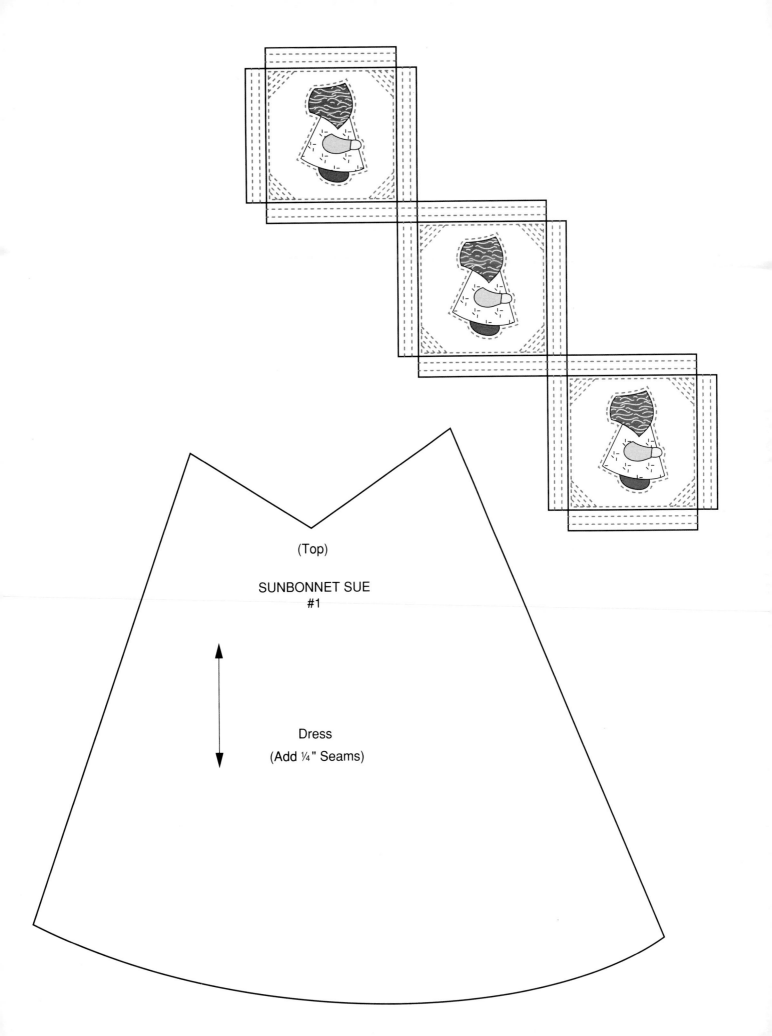

(Top)

SUNBONNET SUE
#1

Dress

(Add ¼" Seams)

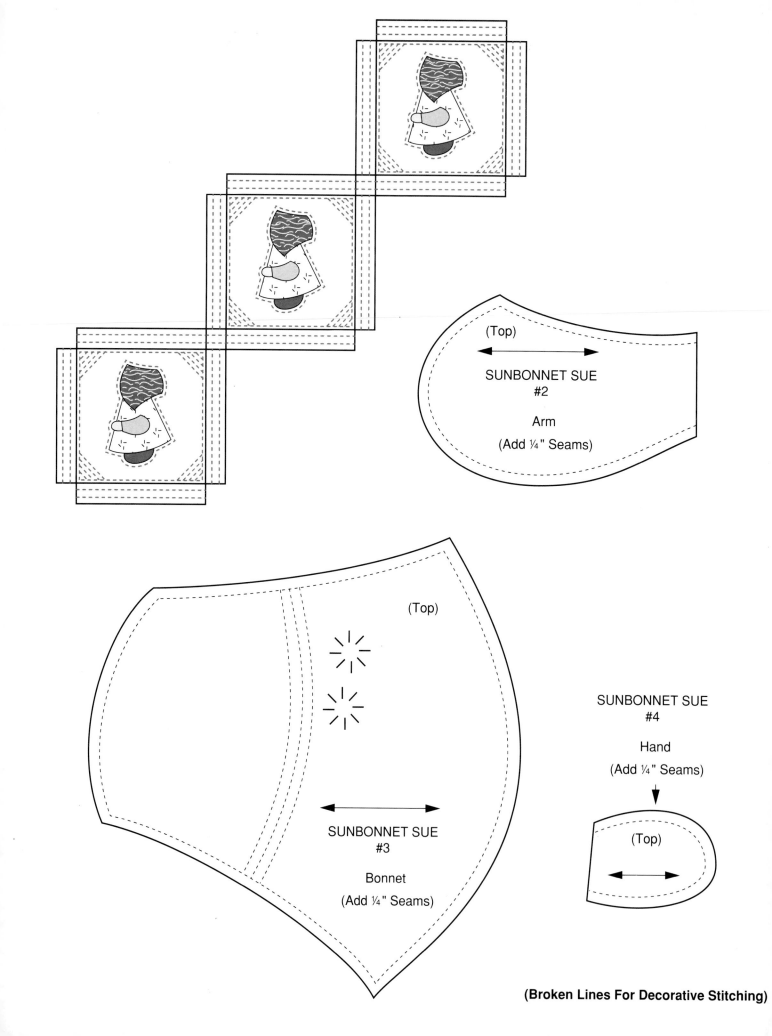

(Top)

SUNBONNET SUE
#2

Arm

(Add ¼" Seams)

(Top)

SUNBONNET SUE
#3

Bonnet

(Add ¼" Seams)

SUNBONNET SUE
#4

Hand

(Add ¼" Seams)

(Top)

(Broken Lines For Decorative Stitching)

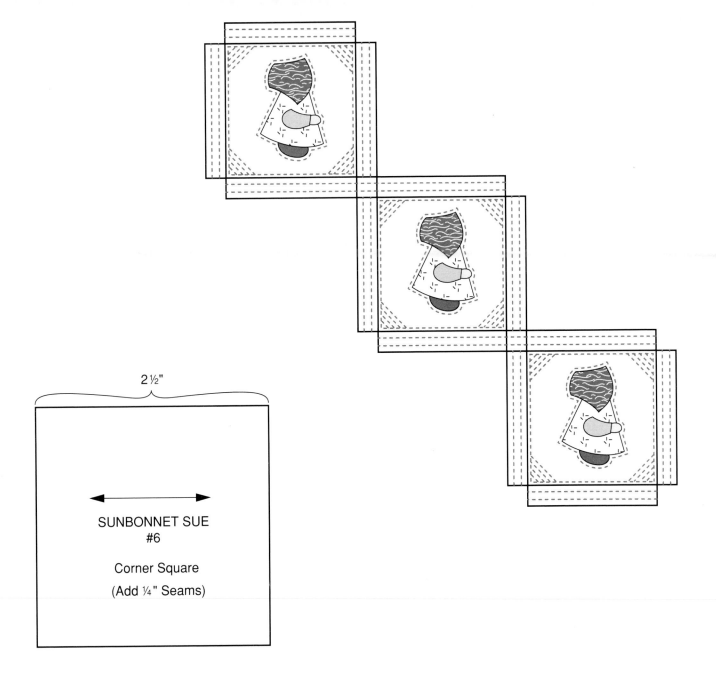

2½"

SUNBONNET SUE
#6

Corner Square

(Add ¼" Seams)

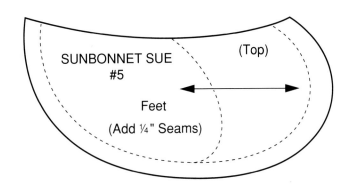

SUNBONNET SUE
#5

(Top)

Feet

(Add ¼" Seams)

(Broken Lines For Decorative Stitching)

THE PERENNIAL FAVORITE
(ROSE OF SHARON)
QUILT BY THE AUTHOR

THE PERENNIAL FAVORITE

There is no denying that the Rose of Sharon is a traditional favorite. It always surfaces as a preference, often over other more elaborate or innovative quilts. It has been dubbed a "perennial" favorite, a fitting description for a rose quilt, perennial meaning "continuing or lasting for years."

The Rose of Sharon has appeared in many variations in American quilt design. And it has often been used as a central motif in larger quilt designs. Quiltmakers often incorporated calico prints with the usual solid shades of pink and green. Marquerite Ickis included the Rose of Sharon pattern in her 1949 book, *The Standard Book of Quiltmaking and Collecting*. Other authors have noted the numerous name variations for the Biblical Rose of Sharon. Both time and geographic movement are reflected in names like Tudor Rose, Whig Rose, Victorian Rose, Ohio Rose, Cherokee Rose, and Prairie Rose.

In her *Garden of Quilts* book, Mary Elizabeth Johnson confirms the popularity of all flower quilts. She notes that "the appeal of flower quilts continues undiminished to this day; contemporary designers draw as much delight from floral motifs as did our ancestors." She further points out that "there are more flower quilts than any other kind. There's hardly a blossom, large or small, that has escaped the quilter's notice." The pattern section of her book includes ten rose design variations.

The rose's popularity is presumably related to its familiarity. People can readily identify with the rose, a favorite garden flower. They like the natural green and rosy hues and the traditional pure white background. Viewers are comfortable with "natural" interpretations in quilts. Unadulterated blossoms, stems, leaves, and buds have their own comprehensive appeal.

My Rose of Sharon quilt is the closest I've come to making a traditional "marriage quilt" – traditional in pattern and color and traditional in the execution of continuous hand-quilted borders of interlocking rings and heart motifs. The delicate latticework design continues unbroken around all the blocks and around every corner. The heart and flower quilted border continues harmoniously around each corner. This border continuity is believed by some to be a predictor of stability in marriage. Broken borders would foretell a broken marriage.

My Rose of Sharon has garnered awards in a National Quilting Association show and the Wisconsin State Historical Museum quilt contest. In a recent retrospective showing of my quilts, it was clearly a viewer's choice, edging out more complex and innovative pieces. The Roses's soothing colors, gently rounded lines, and prodigious quilting all help to lure the onlooker. When it comes to the viewing public, Rose of Sharon is proof positive that natural themes, applique, and, above all, tradition, are still the all-time favorites.

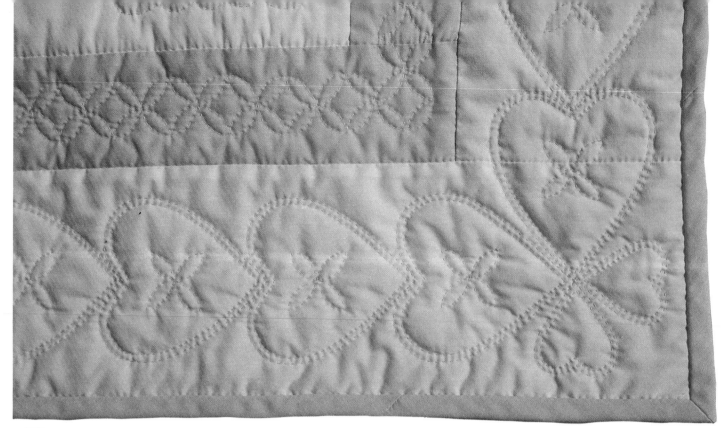

ROSE OF SHARON

FOR STARTERS

The following list will help you enjoy a smooth start and steady progress in your work on the Rose of Sharon quilt. It contains a variety of general information about making the quilt:

- Wash and press all fabrics before you begin.
- Four (4) fabrics are required: green, white, and two shades of pink.
- Hand applique is recommended for this quilt. Use the method of your choice.
- Scant ¼" "turn-under" allowances (about 3⁄16") are recommended for applique pieces.
- Use ¼" seams for piecing the blocks, latticework, and borders.
- For templates (patterns of the quilt pieces) use sturdy plastic, cardboard, or sandpaper, and be sure to note grain lines.
- Twelve (12) appliqued blocks are needed.
- Placement of the pink fabrics on the flowers varies from block to block.

- Each appliqued block measures 20" square, finished.
- The pink latticework is 2½" wide, the white border 6", finished.
- The finished size for the Rose of Sharon quilt is 82" x 104½".

SUPPLIES

Use 44"/45" cotton or cotton/ polyester blend fabrics.

Quilt Top:

Dark Pink: 2¼ yards
Light Pink: ¾ yards
Green: ¾ yard
White: 7 yards

Binding: Buy an additional 1 yard of dark pink.

Backing: 6½ yards of white

Batting: Use a 90" x 108" (queen-size) bonded polyester batt.

OTHER SUPPLIES:

- Iron
- Material for templates
- Marking pencils or soap chips
- Scissors (for paper and fabric)
- Rulers
- Thread for piecing
- Pins

- Pink and green thread for applique
- Thread or safety pins for basting
- Quilting needles
- Pink and white quilting thread
- Thimble
- Long straightedge
- Hoop or frame for quilting

READY TO WORK

COLOR KEY
DP=Dark Pink
LP= Light Pink
G= Green
W= White

TEMPLATES
Begin by making templates of all six Rose of Sharon pattern pieces (1, 2, 3, 4, 5, 6). Note that scant ¼" turn under allowances must be added to all applique pieces.

CUTTING
Begin with the Dark Pink (DP) fabric. Cut the following lattice pieces (seam allowances included):
Cut 5 cross lattices 3" x 70½"
Cut 16 short strips 3" x 20½"
Then cut the following (DP) applique pieces:

Cut 6 of Template #1 (center)

Cut 24 of Template #2 (inner petal)

Cut 24 of Template #3 (outer petal)

Cut 24 of Template #6 (bud)

Cut the following pieces from the Light Pink (LP) fabric:

Cut 6 of Template #1 (center)

Cut 24 of Template #2 (inner petal)

Cut 24 of Template #3 (outer petal)

Cut 24 of Template #6 (bud)

From the Green (G) fabric:

Cut 48 of Template #4 (leaves)

Cut 48 of Template #5 (stem)

Continue with the White (W) fabric and cut the following (allowances for seams included):

Cut 2 side borders 6½" x 93"

Cut 2 end borders 6½" x 82½"

Cut 12 squares 20½" x 20½"

APPLIQUE

Collect the 21 applique pieces for a block with a dark pink (DP) center. Turn under a scant ¼" on each piece. It is NOT necessary to turn under the edges marked with an "X" on the pattern pieces (the inner edges of the petal pieces, the short end of the stem and leaf, and the rounded end of the bud), as these will be tucked behind adjacent applique pieces.

Fold the background square into quarters and press lightly to locate and mark the center and quarter division lines. Place the applique pieces on the square, according to Diagram 1.

Place a dark pink (DP) circle in the center and pin in place. Place 4 light pink (LP) small petals around it, each centered on a crease line. Tuck the petals under the center circle and pin in place.

Likewise, place 4 dark pink (DP) large petals on the block, with the inner edges tucked under the smaller petals. Place leaves, stems, and dark pink (DP) buds in a similar manner. The points of the buds should clear the outer edge of the

Diagram 1

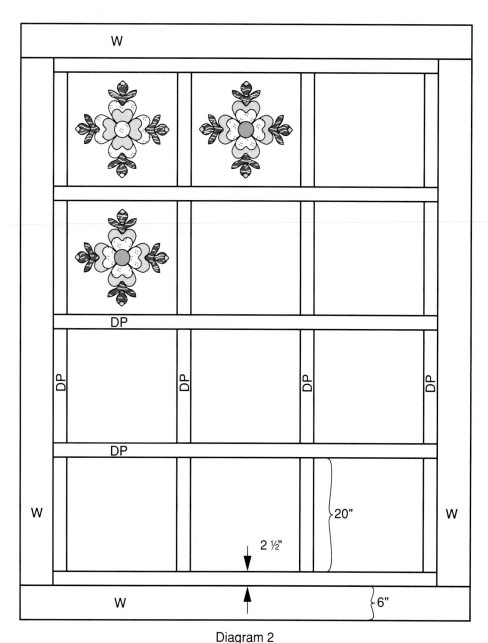

Diagram 2

Diagram 3

square by at least ¾".

Baste all pieces to the background square. Then applique around all pieces, using small even blind stitches. Use pink thread around centers, petals, and buds. Use green thread around stems and leaves. Make 5 more similar blocks with Dark Pink (DP) centers. Then make 6 blocks with the Light Pink (LP) centers and alternate color placement of petals and buds.

LATTICEWORK and BORDERS

Refer to Diagram 2 for the general layout of the quilt top. Place the appliqued flowers with light and dark centers alternating. For Row 1, piece 3 appliqued blocks and 4 Dark Pink (DP) short strips, as in Diagram 3. Make similar panels for Rows 2, 3, 4.

Add a long Dark Pink (DP) cross lattice between the rows and at the top and bottom, according to Diagram 2. Add the white borders to complete the quilt top.

THE FINISHING TOUCH

QUILTING

From the 6½ yards of white backing fabric, cut two 3¼ yard lengths. Keep one intact (about 42" wide). From the other piece, cut two 21" widths. Join a 21" width to each side of the intact center panel. Press seams toward the outside.

Place the quilt backing right side down on a large flat surface. Smooth the batting over it. Place the pressed quilt top over the batting, right side up. Carefully pin or thread baste the three layers together for quilting.

With a washable marking pencil, mark the quilting Designs 1, 2, 3, and 4 on the squares, latticework, and borders. Use Design 1 in the four corners of each block. Use Design 2 in the latticework. Use Designs 3 and 4 in the outer borders.

Quilt close to the seam around all applique pieces and blocks. Quilt Designs 1, 3, and 4 (block and borders) with pink thread. Quilt Design 2 (latticework) with white thread.

BINDING

Trim the batting to ½" larger than the quilt top, to allow for filler in the binding. Trim the batting to match the top. From the 1 yard of pink binding fabric, make 3" wide continuous bias binding.

Fold the binding in half lengthwise, wrong sides together. Then attach it to the quilt front in a seam that penetrates all the layers. Turn the binding to the back and whipstitch it in place.

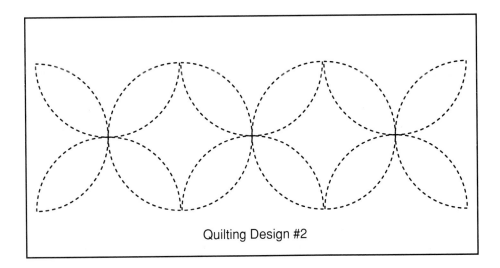

Quilting Design #2

Quilting Design #1

Quilting Design #3

Quilting Design #4

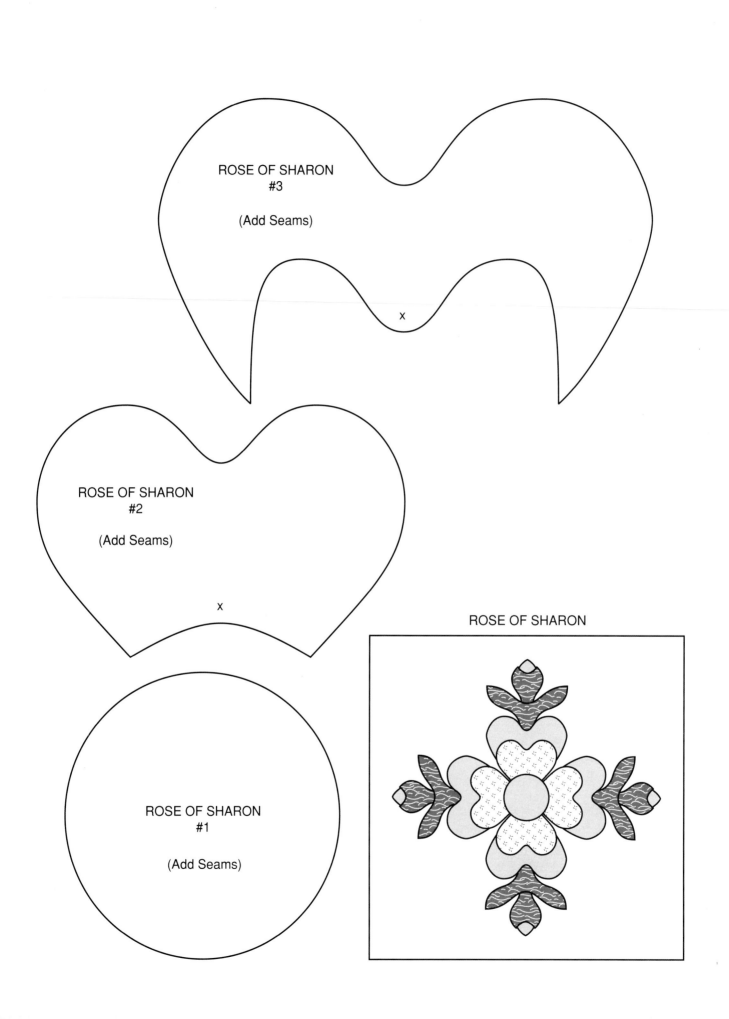

ROSE OF SHARON
#3

(Add Seams)

x

ROSE OF SHARON
#2

(Add Seams)

x

ROSE OF SHARON

ROSE OF SHARON
#1

(Add Seams)

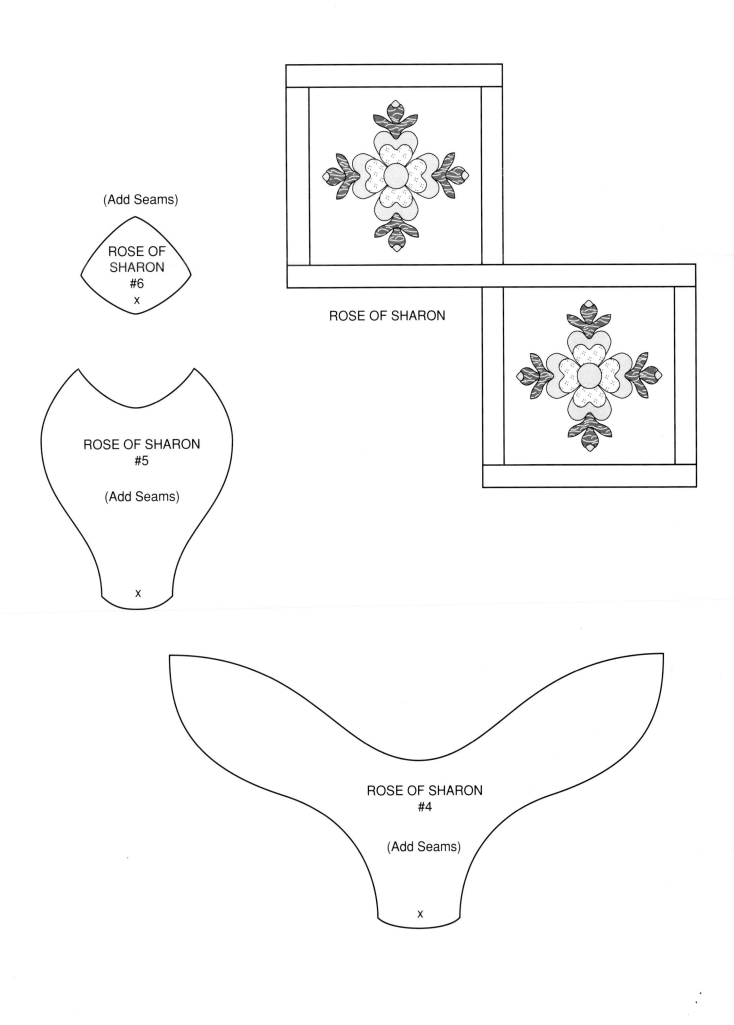

(Add Seams)

ROSE OF
SHARON
#6
x

ROSE OF SHARON

ROSE OF SHARON
#5

(Add Seams)

x

ROSE OF SHARON
#4

(Add Seams)

x

MY STARS! A COMPUTER QUILT
(STAR APPLIQUE)
QUILT BY PAT SIMONSEN
Based On A Computer Design Program By Jim Simonsen, Eau Claire, Wisconsin

MY STARS! A COMPUTER QUILT

The notion of using a computer with quiltmaking probably boggles most quilters. Others are fascinated, even amazed by the new developments in computer quilt design. If you own or have access to a computer, you might consider trying the software available for quilt designs, if only for inspiration and experimentation.

Although computers cannot make your fabric selections in a quilt shop, mark your design on the fabric, or even thread your needle, they are good for two things: ideas and saving time. Quiltmakers need not shy away from the idea of sharing their work space with a computer. Don't be intimidated by the mechanics and jargon of a computer. View it as a modern day tool, alongside your rotary cutter, electric pencil sharpener, and VCR.

Pat and Jim Simonsen have been exploring computer quilt designs for nearly ten years. Rectangles, squares, triangles, stars and circles have graced the screen of their computer monitor.

Jim has created a program that explores quilt designs based on rectangles, equilateral triangles, and overlapping circles. Options for varying sizes, placement, and colors are included. Other features include special graph paper design printouts and yardage calculations for selected designs.

Pat has successfully converted several of their designs into fabrics. Her pieced computer wall quilts feature six-point stars and isometric triangles. Her applique success is pictured here. "My Stars! A Computer Quilt" is from an overlapping circle pattern reminiscent of the traditional Double Wedding Ring. Other circular computer designs go far beyond the basic ring structure, with formation of intricate secondary shapes.

Pat selected a fairly uncomplicated design for her quilt, a design that lends itself readily to applique, without the hassle of concave curves and tiny pieces. She used a wide array of fabrics in a monochromatic blue theme. Each star is appliqued with a different blue fabric, adding texture and depth to her "starry" arrangement.

Pat adds her personal touch by expanding on the stellar theme. Astronomy is not just a passing interest for the Simonsen family. It is also an area of expertise for Jim, a physicist by profession. So the phenomenon of star development and variability was a natural thing to include in the quilt design. The "white dwarf," the initial formation of a new celestial body, is reflected in the small block with the white center. The familiar "red giant" or exploding star in its final stages of observable development, holds a prominent place on her quilt.

"My Stars! A Computer Quilt" has captured the attention of quilt designers and judges. It has garnered several honors at Midwest quilt shows. It was juried into the American Quilter's Society Quilt Show & Contest in Paducah, Kentucky. And it was featured in the AQS *Quilt Art '89* engagement calendar. Probably Pat's unequaled honor was in presenting the quilt to her daughter, Julie, on the occasion of her high school graduation.

Pat excels in many areas of quiltmaking. Computer designing is just one of her areas of expertise. One of her pieced designs, the "Christmas Ribbons" wall quilt, is included elsewhere in this book.

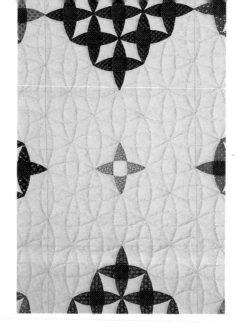

My stars!
A COMPUTER QUILT

FOR STARTERS

The following list will help you enjoy a smooth start and steady progress in your work on the Computer quilt. It contains a variety of general information about making the quilt.

- Wash and press all fabrics before you begin.
- A variety of blue print fabrics (up to thirty) is needed for this quilt.
- Hand applique is recommended for the quilt. Use the method of your choice.
- Scant ¼" "turn-under" allowances (about ³⁄₁₆") are recommended for applique pieces.
- The "stars" are appliqued on to light blue background blocks.
- Use ¼" seams for piecing the blocks together.
- Only two templates are required.
- For templates (patterns of the quilt pieces) use sturdy plastic, cardboard, or sandpaper, and be sure to note grain lines.
- The directions are for a quilt exactly like the one pictured here, including the two star "variations."
- The finished size for the Computer Stars quilt is 70" x 84".

SUPPLIES

Use 44"/45" wide cotton or cotton/polyester blend fabrics.

Quilt Top:
Blue Prints: ¼ yard EACH of 30 fabrics or scraps
Dark Blue Pin Dot (for star centers and binding): 2 yards
Red Pin Dot: ⅛ yard
White Solid: ⅛ yard, OR a fabric scrap about 3" square
Light Blue: 4¾ yards
Binding: (Included in Dark Blue Pin Dot above)
Backing: 5½ yards good quality unbleached muslin
Batting: Use a 72" x 90" (twin-size) bonded polyester batt

OTHER SUPPLIES

- Iron
- Material for templates
- Marking pencils or soap chips
- Scissors (for paper and fabric)
- Rulers
- Blue, red, and white thread for applique
- Light blue thread for piecing
- Pins
- Thread or safety pins for basting
- Quilting needles
- 2 spools light blue quilting thread
- Thimble
- Hoop or frame for quilting

READY TO WORK

COLOR KEY
P= Blue Prints
DB= Dark Blue Pin Dot
R= Red Pin Dot
W= White
LB= Light Blue

TEMPLATES
Begin by making templates of the two Computer Stars pattern pieces (Templates #1 and 2). Note that the scant ¼" turn under allowances must be added to each piece.

CUTTING
Begin with the Blue Print (P) fabrics. Select 2 fabrics to be used for the "red giant" and "white dwarf" blocks and set these aside. From each of the remaining 28 fabrics, you will need to cut 18 using Template 1. Be sure to adhere to the suggested grain line and add the turn-under allowances.

From the fabric designated for the "red giant" block, cut 26 of

Template 1. From the fabric designated for the "white dwarf" block, cut 2 of Template 1.

Continue with the Dark Blue Pin Dot (DB) fabric. Cut a total of 252 of Template 2 for the star centers. Set the remaining (DB) fabric aside for the binding.

From the White (W) fabric, cut 1 of Template 2 for the "white dwarf" block.

From the Red Pin Dot (R) fabric, cut 13 from Template 2 for the "red giant" block.

From the Light Blue (LB) fabric, cut 30 background squares, each 14½" x 14½" (seams included).

PUTTING IT TOGETHER
APPLIQUE

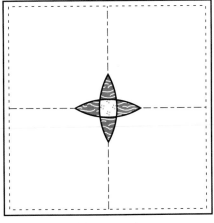

Diagram 1

Collect the 27 pieces needed for one block – 18 oval pieces and 9 centers. Turn under a scant ¼" around all edges of each piece.

Fold a background square in quarters and press lightly to make crease lines marking the center and 4 quadrants. Place the 2 oval pieces for the middle of the star in the center of the background block, as in Diagram 1. Place the small Blue Pin Dot piece on top of them, in the center. Pin all three pieces in place.

Continue to add the other pieces to complete the design as shown in Diagram 2. Be sure that the ends of the ovals do not extend into the ¼" seam allowances of the background block. They should just come close to it.

Baste all of the pieces to the background block. Then applique around all pieces using small even blind stitches. Use dark blue thread around the centers and blue thread to match the print fabrics. Make a total of 28 applique blocks with Dark Blue centers.

For the "red giant" block, increase the applique pieces to 26 blue print ovals and 13 red centers. Place the pieces like the blocks above, adding another unit in each corner, as in Diagram 3.

For the "white dwarf" block,

applique only 2 blue print ovals and 1 white center onto a background block, as in Diagram 4.

ASSEMBLY

After all 30 blocks have been appliqued, lay all the blocks on a

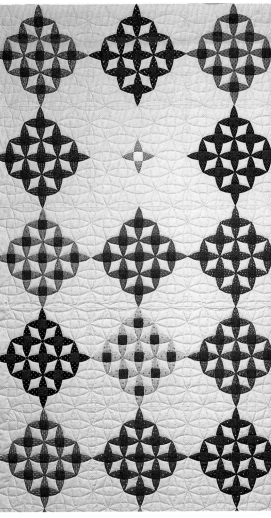

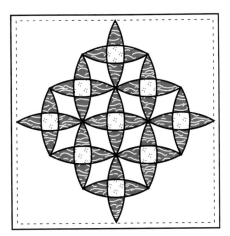

Diagram 2

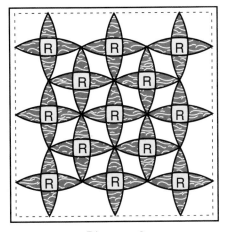

Diagram 3

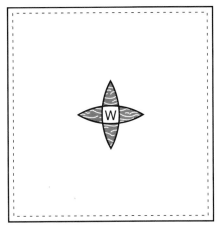

Diagram 4

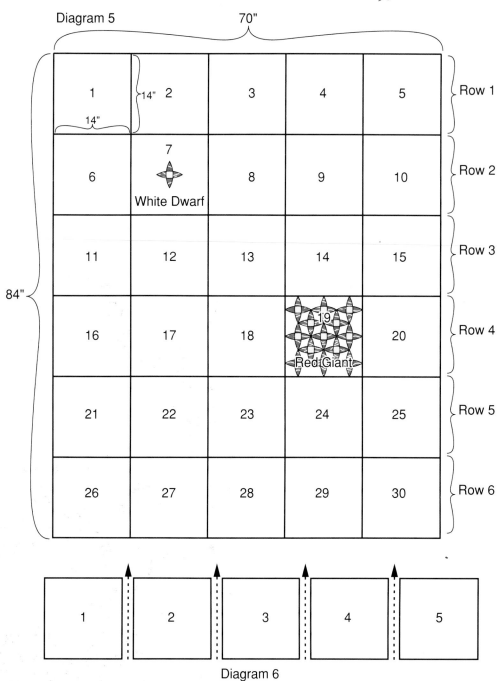

Diagram 5   70"

Row 1

1 | 14" 2 | 3 | 4 | 5

14"

Row 2

6 | 7 White Dwarf | 8 | 9 | 10

Row 3

11 | 12 | 13 | 14 | 15

84"

Row 4

16 | 17 | 18 | 19 Red Giant | 20

Row 5

21 | 22 | 23 | 24 | 25

Row 6

26 | 27 | 28 | 29 | 30

1 | 2 | 3 | 4 | 5

Diagram 6

Diagram 7

large flat surface and arrange them according to your preference. Refer to Diagram 5 and the color photograph for suggestions. Number and label the blocks, #1 through 30.

Piece the 5 blocks that comprise Row 1 together in short vertical seams, as in Diagram 6. Piece Rows 2 through 6 in a similar way. Join the rows together in long horizontal cross seams to complete the top.

THE FINISHING TOUCH

QUILTING

From the 5½ yards of muslin backing fabric, cut two, 2¾ yard lengths. Keep one intact (about 42" wide). From the other piece, cut two 21" widths. Join a 21" width to each side of the intact center panel. Press seams toward the outside.

Place the quilt backing fabric right side down on a large flat sur-

face. Smooth the batting over it. Place the pressed quilt top over the batting, right side up. Pin or thread baste the three layers together for quilting.

Use light blue quilting thread to quilt "in-the-ditch" around each applique piece, as suggested in Diagram 7.

Use a washable marking pencil and the oval template to mark the curved shapes (Quilting Design #1) in the light blue background areas around each applique star. The marked shapes should meet and continue on to adjacent blocks. The result will be a sequence of curved lines that echo the shape of the applique pieces, as suggested in Diagram 8.

BINDING

Trim the batting to ½" larger than the quilt top, to allow for filler in the binding. Trim the backing to match the top. From the remaining 1 yard of Dark Blue Pin Dot fabric, make 3" wide continuous bias binding.

Fold the binding in half lengthwise, wrong sides together. Attach it to the quilt front in a seam that penetrates all layers. Turn the binding to the back and whipstitch it in place.

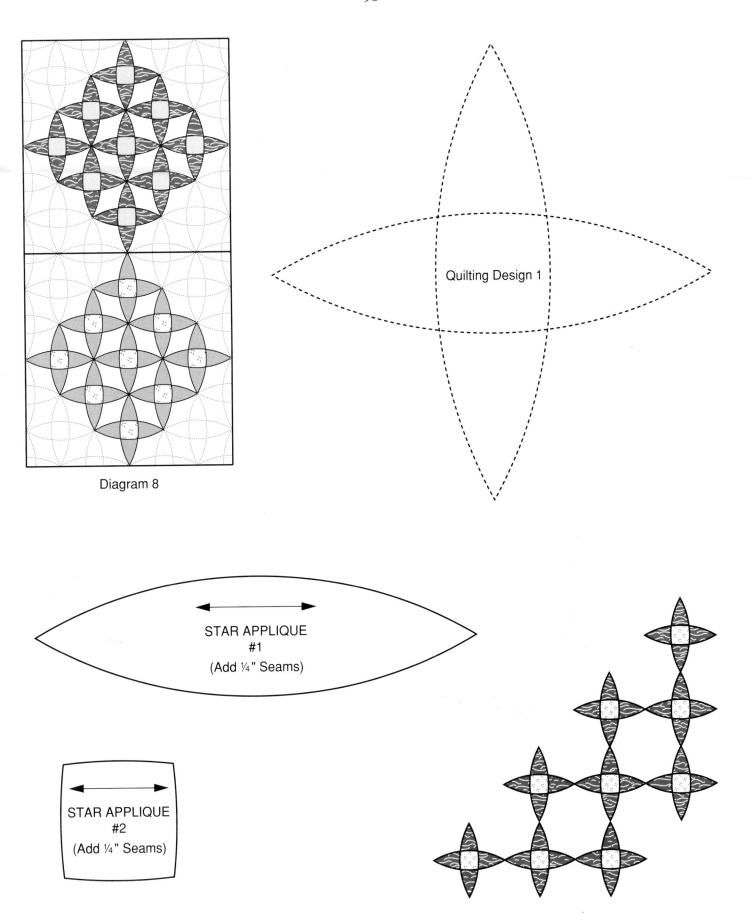

Diagram 8

Quilting Design 1

STAR APPLIQUE
#1
(Add ¼" Seams)

STAR APPLIQUE
#2
(Add ¼" Seams)

SIXTY YEARS LATER AND STILL QUILTING
(FRENCH BASKET)
QUILT BY MARIE HALMSTAD, EAU CLAIRE, WISCONSIN

SIXTY YEARS LATER AND STILL QUILTING

An intricate applique quilt may not be the customary choice for a 17-year-old's first quilt. But back in 1929, when Marie Halmstad saw a neighbor lady's pattern for the French Basket* quilt, she knew she wanted to make one for her hope chest. Marie copied the pattern on brown butcher paper and headed for the general store in her Stanley, Wisconsin hometown.

Marie remembers buying the popular Peter Pan cotton materials in the dry goods department. She did all the hand applique. ("The border was a little difficult," she recalls.) Blocks and borders were pieced on a treadle Singer.

Marie called it her "basket of wild roses" and quilted it in 1929-30, her last year in high school. She recalls "We had it on a great big frame in the living room. I loved to sew. I enjoy doing handwork." Marie added the quilt to her hope chest along with her embroidered items. "I thought it was something pretty wonderful at the time," she recalls.

Marriage and family soon followed and Marie's French Basket moved from the hope chest to the bed. "It was the only bedspread I had during the depression years. I get just sick when I think how I washed it and then hung it on a rope clothesline. When it started to wear, I thought 'Oh you can't have a raggedy thing like that on the bed,' so I stopped using it, wrapped it in a sheet, and put it in a box." It stayed there for many years.

Sixty years have passed since Marie made her first quilt. She is now nearly eighty years old. Her interest in quilts has been rekindled. She has been piecing, quilting, and designing quilts steadily since 1980. A Sampler, a Capital T, a Kaleidoscope, a Round the Twist, and a Ships quilt have all passed through her frame. Her Nine Patch Churn Dash quilt is featured in my book *Award-Winning Quick Quilts*.

Marie now uses template plastic instead of brown butcher paper. She uses a revolving, tiltable circular frame in place of the four-board, C-clamp apparatus. And the treadle sewing machine has a modern replacement.

Marie takes her French Basket quilt out of the box for occasional use and special showings. "It's a little sad. I often think of the depression when I look at the quilt now," she says. "But I appreciate it more now, when I think how much work went into it. And it sure held. That thread sure held up in all that time. I'm happy I used it."

*The French Basket pattern was originally designed in 1915 for The "Ladies' Home Journal" when Marie D. Webster was needlework editor. It was later available in stamped kits, basted versions, and finished quilts. In the 1930's Mrs. Scioto Danner of Kansas offered a similar pattern called The Ivory Basket through her mail-order pattern service.

FRENCH BASKET

FOR STARTERS

The following list will help you enjoy a smooth start and steady progress in your work on the French Basket. It contains a variety of general information about making the quilt:

- Wash and press all fabrics before you begin.
- A minimum of 6 solid color fabrics is required: blue, green, white, yellow, light pink, and dark pink.
- Scant ¼" seams are recommended for applique pieces.
- For templates (patterns of the pieces), use sturdy plastic, cardboard, or sandpaper, and be sure to note grain lines.
- The French Basket quilt requires hand applique techniques. Use the applique method of your choice.

- Thirty (30) applique blocks are needed: 15 white baskets on blue fabric and 15 white blocks with decorative blue edging and ribbon work.
- A streamlined method for making the bias basket handles and the decorative blue ribbon work is included.
- Each block measures 12 inches square, finished.
- The borders are 6" wide and feature appliqued flowers and blue edging.
- The finished size for the French Basket quilt is 72" x 84".

SUPPLIES

Use 44"/45" wide cotton or cotton/ polyester blend fabrics.

Quilt Top:
  White: 6 yards
  Blue: 6½ yards
  Green: 1¼ yards
  Yellow: ⅛ yard
  Light Pink: ¼ yard
  Dark Print: ½ yard

Binding: (Included in the blue fabric above)

Backing: 5½ yards of good quality white muslin

Batting: Use an 81" x 96" (double-size) bonded polyester batt.

OTHER SUPPLIES

- Iron
- Material for templates
- Paper for applique
- Marking pencils or soap chips
- Scissors (for paper and fabric)

- Rulers
- Thread for applique, in colors to match the 6 fabrics
- White or blue thread for piecing blocks and borders
- Pins
- Thread or safety pins for basting
- 2 spools white quilting thread
- Quilting needles
- Thimble
- Long straightedge
- Hoop or frame for quilting

READY TO WORK

COLOR KEY

W= White
B= Blue
G= Green
Y= Yellow
LP= Light Pink
DP=Dark Pink

TEMPLATES

Begin by making templates of the thirteen French Basket pattern pieces (#1 through #13). Mark the grain lines which are indicated on some of the patterns. Note that seam allowances must be added on all sides of each piece. For applique, a scant ¼" seam (closer to ³/₁₆") is recommended.

CUTTING

Begin with the White (W) fabric. First, cut the following borders and background blocks. Allowances for seams and mitering are included for the borders and the background blocks:

Cut 2 side borders 6½" x 84½"
Cut 2 end borders 6½" x 72½"
Cut 15 background blocks each 12½" x 12½"

Next, cut 15 basket pieces from Template 1, adding seams. Set aside the remaining White (W) fabric to be used later for the bias basket handles.

Continue with the Blue (B) fabric and cut the following:

Cut 15 background blocks each 12½" x 12½" (seams included)
Cut 104 of Template 12
Cut 8 of Template 13 (corner edging)

Set aside the remaining Blue (B) fabric for the bias ribbon work and the outer binding.

Next, cut the following applique pieces from the Green (G) fabric:

Cut 59 of Template 6 (stem/leaf)
Cut 15 of Template 7 (curved stem/leaf)
Cut 133 of Template 8 (leaf)
Cut 30 of Template 9 (short stem)
Cut 30 of Template 10 (long stem)

From the Yellow (Y) fabric, cut the following pieces:

Cut 37 of Template 4 (flower center)

From the Light Pink (LP) fabric, cut the following pieces:

Cut 30 of Template 11 (flower)

From the Dark Pink (DP) fabric, cut the following pieces:

Cut 37 of Template 2 (petal)
Cut 37 of Template 3 (petal)
Cut 37 of Template 5 (petal)

PUTTING IT TOGETHER

BASKET APPLIQUE

Begin by making the bias strips for the basket handles. To make bias from the remaining white fabric, cut true bias strips 1 inch wide and about 18 inches long (see Diagram 1). For each basket you will need 2 strips, so you need a total of 30, 18-inch strips for the quilt. These may be pieced if necessary (to make

them 18").

Fold each bias strip in half lengthwise, with wrong sides together and raw edges even. Sew a ⅛" seam, stitching the length of the 18" strip, as in Diagram 2. Roll the stitched strip so the seam is centered, as in Diagram 3. Press the seam open.

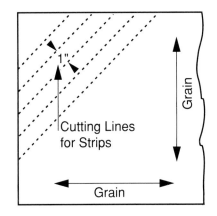

Diagram 1: Making Bias Strips

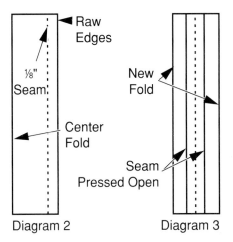

Diagram 2   Diagram 3

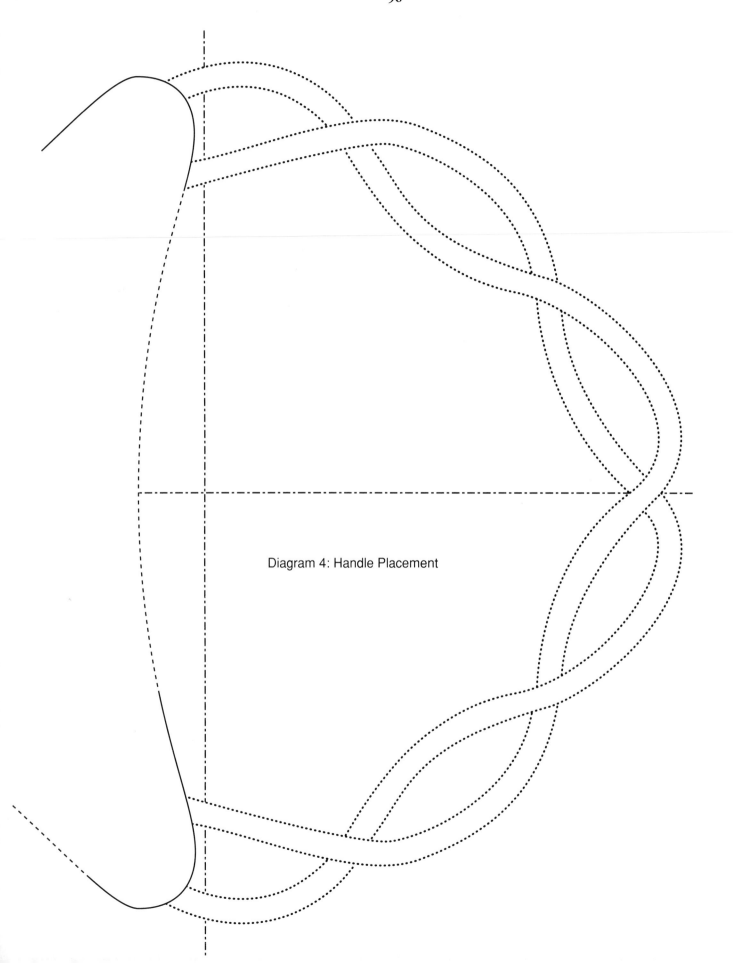

Diagram 4: Handle Placement

Diagram 5: Flower Placement

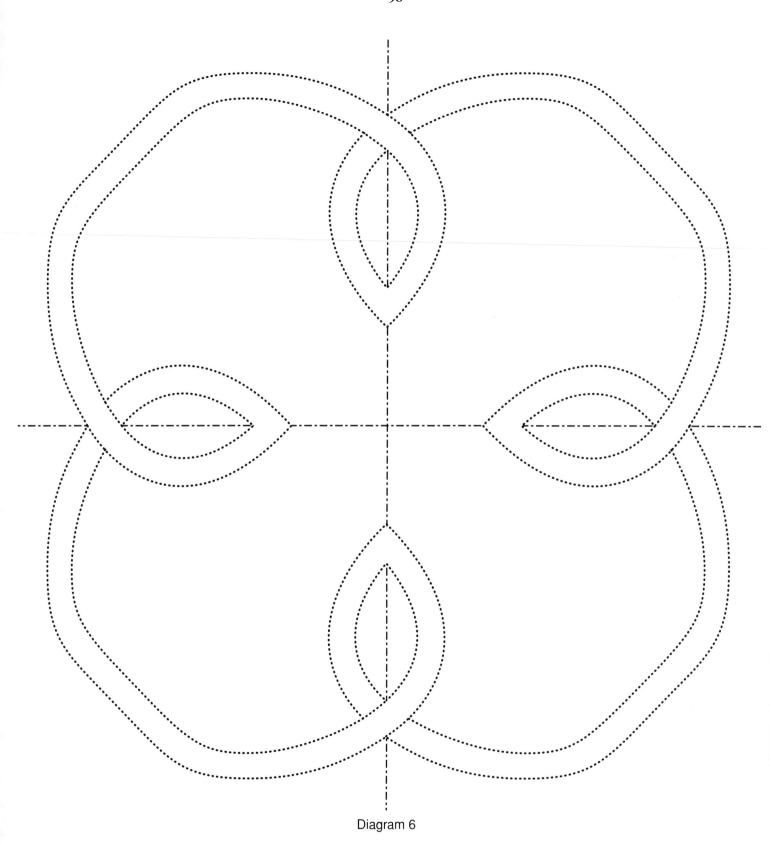

Diagram 6

Fold a blue background block in half in both directions, to locate and mark the center and quarter sections. Press the folds lightly. (Folds are indicated by broken lines in Diagram 4, 5, and 6.)

Place two bias strips on the background block, along the dotted lines indicated for the basket handle, referring to Diagram 4. Pin in place.

Next, pin the basket (#1) to the background block, using Diagram 5 as your guide. Turn under the seam allowances of the basket. Tuck the handles behind the basket. Applique with small invisible stitches.

Carefully cut a slit in each of the five openings in the basket. Turn under to the lines indicated on the pattern, trimming and clipping if necessary. This procedure is similar to a reverse applique method.

Next, pin and applique the flowers, stems, and leaves in place, using Diagram 5 as your guide.

Complete the 15 baskets.

BACKGROUND BLOCKS

Begin by making bias strips from the remaining Blue (B) fabric. You will need a length to total about 55" for each block. Use the same procedure and diagrams given for making the white bias basket handles above. Cut bias strips 1" wide and as long as the fabric permits. Piece these segments to lengths of about 55". Then fold, stitch, and press according to Diagrams 1, 2, and 3. You will need 15, 55" blue strips.

To complete a background block, pin the blue bias strip according to the lines indicated in Diagram 6. Trim and miter the points (to reduce bulk). Applique in place.

Pin a blue edge piece (Template 12) on each side of the white block, about 1½" from the corners of the block. Applique in place. Make 15 such blocks.

Complete the quilt top center by piecing together the 30 appliqued blocks according to Diagram 7.

BORDER APPLIQUE

All border applique pieces must be carefully placed in order to match the adjacent appliqued blocks.

Begin with the end (top and bottom) borders. Fold the border piece in half, to locate the center. Then mark the center 12" interval where the bottom center appliqued block will be attached. Mark two, 12" intervals on each side (a total of 5, 12" intervals), as in Diagram 8.

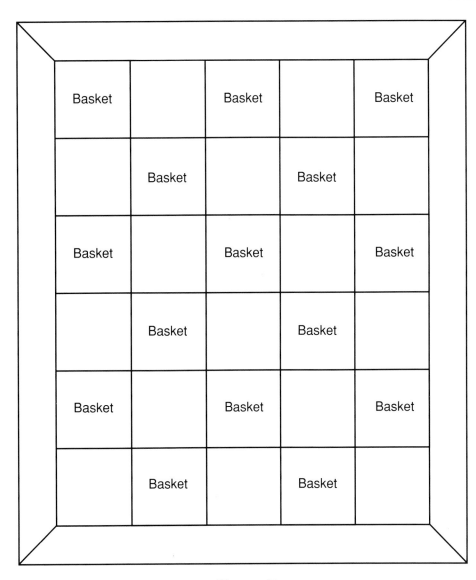

Diagram 7

Diagram 8: End Border

These intervals will match the seams in the appliqued block section.

Pin a blue edge piece (Template 12) in the center section, as shown in Diagram 8. Applique. Add blue edge pieces in the center of the other 4 marked intervals. Then add edge pieces directly across from these 5 pieces, along the outer edge of the border. Add corner edging pieces (Template 13) in each corner, for a total of 7 blue edge pieces along the outer edge.

Next, arrange the 4 flower clusters according to Diagram 9. Place these in the open white areas between the blue edge pieces. Applique the flowers in place.

Make another end border.

To make the side borders, follow a similar procedure. The main difference is that the side borders are longer and require 6 blue edge pieces on the inner edge and 8 blue edge pieces along the outer edge. Five applique flower clusters are needed.

ADDING THE BORDERS

Add the top and bottom borders, being careful to match the blue edge pieces. Begin and end the stitching to allow for mitered corners. Then add the side borders. Miter the corners.

Then arrange the 4 corner flowers, as shown in Diagram 10. Place these in the corners, on top of the mitered seams.

THE FINISHING TOUCH

QUILTING

From the 5½ yards of white backing fabric, cut two .2¾-yard lengths. Keep one intact (about 42" wide). From the other piece, cut two 21-inch widths. Join a 21" width to each side of the intact center panel. Press seams toward the outside.

Place the quilt backing right side down on a large flat surface. Smooth the batting over it. Place the pressed quilt top over the batting, right side up. Pin or thread baste the three layers together for quilting.

Use a washable marking pencil and a long straightedge (or masking tape) to mark diagonal parallel quilting lines on all blocks and borders. Mark lines about an inch apart, in both directions, to form a cross-hatching design. Do not mark lines on the baskets, flowers, leaves or bias strips.

Use white thread to quilt in all the background areas and on edging pieces. Also, quilt just inside the five openings in each basket.

BINDING

Trim the batting to ½" larger than the quilt top, to allow for filler in the binding. Trim the backing to match the top. From the remaining Blue (B) fabric, make 3" wide continuous bias binding.

Fold the binding in half lengthwise, wrong sides together. Then attach it to the quilt front in a seam that penetrates all the layers. Turn the binding to the back and whipstitch it in place.

Diagram 9: Border Flowers

Diagram 10: Corner Flowers

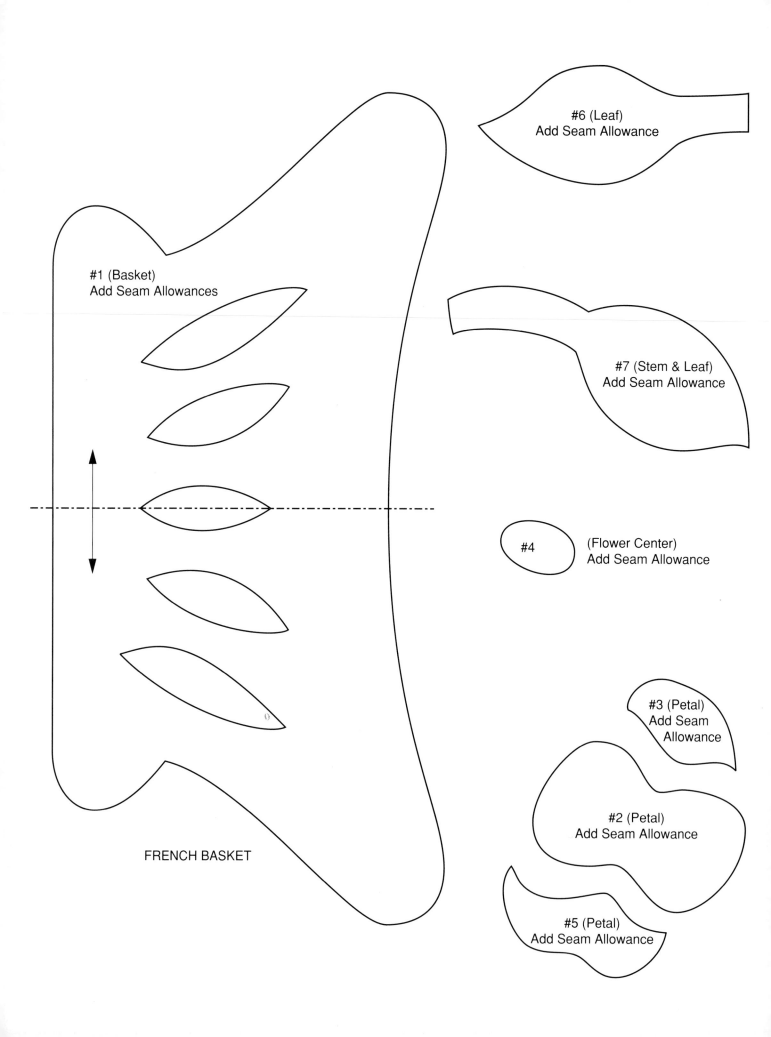

#6 (Leaf)
Add Seam Allowance

#1 (Basket)
Add Seam Allowances

#7 (Stem & Leaf)
Add Seam Allowance

#4   (Flower Center)
Add Seam Allowance

#3 (Petal)
Add Seam
Allowance

#2 (Petal)
Add Seam Allowance

FRENCH BASKET

#5 (Petal)
Add Seam Allowance

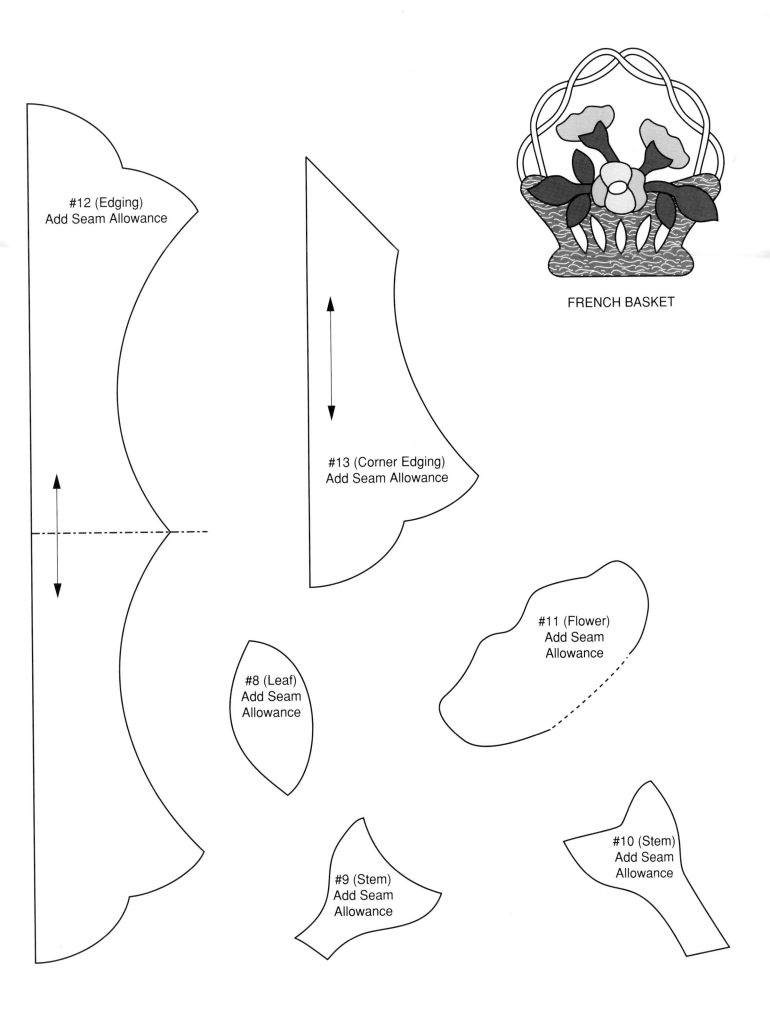

#12 (Edging)
Add Seam Allowance

#13 (Corner Edging)
Add Seam Allowance

FRENCH BASKET

#11 (Flower)
Add Seam
Allowance

#8 (Leaf)
Add Seam
Allowance

#9 (Stem)
Add Seam
Allowance

#10 (Stem)
Add Seam
Allowance

**TWENTY-THREE BIRDS, TWENTY-ONE BUNNIES, EIGHTEEN PUPPIES,
SEVEN WHALES, AND ONE ELEPHANT**
(FAVORITE CREATURES CRIB QUILT)
QUILT BY DAVID FLORENCE AND THE AUTHOR

TWENTY-THREE BIRDS, TWENTY-ONE BUNNIES, EIGHTEEN PUPPIES, SEVEN WHALES, AND ONE ELEPHANT

Many quilt authors have written about the quilt-making traditions that link the generations in families. They point to the multitude of quilts that have served as a network in the formation of bonds between mothers and daughters, aunts and nieces, grandmothers and grand-daughter. They give poignant accounts of women whose quiltmaking has strengthened family connections, of women, who by the simple act of piecing together, sharing a quilt frame, or taking part in a friendship quilt have also renewed and reinforced family ties.

Most authors fail to point out that this phenomenon is not restricted to women, or mothers and daughters. Sons, brothers, fathers, and grandfathers have also been part of this inter-connected past. The male role in the family quilt-making scene, though perhaps a lesser one, has mostly been overlooked.

Men make up the majority in our home. They all appreciate quiltmaking, but up until recently none of them had expressed interest in taking part in it. So when the first traces of interest were revealed, they caught my attention immediately. The factor that triggered the interest was the arrival of a Featherweight sewing machine in our home. The mechanics of the multiple moving parts of this miniature machine, and the jet black and radiant gold decorative lettering could understandably attract the attention of a ten-year-old boy.

And so it did at our house. David not only showed a marked curiosity about the machine, but an express interest in learning how to use it. It seemed that I couldn't get it threaded soon enough to suit him. I spent a few minutes sewing – forward and backward, starting and stopping – satisfied with my own knowledge and basic skill with the Featherweight. David stood hovering over my shoulder, wide-eyed and inquisitive. I offered to let him try his hand at it. He immediately liked it and appeared to be a "natural" with both machine and fabric. The small machine and David's body "fit" together comfortably. The proportions were right. And after just a few practice sessions he had mastered elementary straight line piecing. Shortly, he announced his intention to make a quilt.

I was delighted with his excitement. Here was fresh energy and fascination for quilting right under my own roof. I assured David that, yes, he could certainly make a quilt; that it was a terrific idea, and I'd be glad to help him.

We began to talk about ideas for a quilt. Meanwhile, he practiced sewing on small scraps of fabric, stitching straight lines, carefully measuring and checking for ¼" seams.

We decided to start with a crib-size project. I suggested a rainbow color theme using leftover pastel fabrics from my previous quilts. We collected all the light solid scraps to see what we had – blues, yellows, pinks, lavenders, greens, and aquas. We chose the simplest of shapes – a square – and began cutting pieces.

We set up shop on our long kitchen counter – a stack of fabrics, iron and towel, rotary cutter, ruler and mat. All the fabric needed pressing. I showed David how to press them. He took the iron and began to press, scrap after scrap, color by color. Intrigued with the power of steam and spray, he soon transformed the wrinkled mass of cloth into a colorful rainbow array of fabrics.

David pressed and the stack grew higher. I began cutting strips and squares. Reluctantly we would set the iron and cutter aside for other things, like meals, dishes, telephone calls, or homework. But we always resumed pressing and cutting at the earliest opportunity.

After we had accumulated several squares, we spread them on the living room floor, trying different arrangements of shades and colors. We tried organized designs like Trip Around the World and Sunshine and Shadow. We tried nine-patch designs and random layouts. In the end we settled on a random distribution of light colors throughout the center, bound by the deeper colors.

The kitchen counter now became the sewing center. David began piecing, square by square, four-inch blocks into long colorful panels. My job was inspector, checking for even stitching, consistent seam widths, and no inside-out seams. As David sewed, I pressed seams. Finally we pinned and pieced the panels.

Our initial idea for the quilting design was a favorite "thing" quilted on each square. We also considered an alphabet theme. The enormity of the task of custom designing 70 "favorite things" and the challenge of arranging a 26-letter alphabet on a 70-block quilt soon discouraged us from thoses ideas.

We settled on a "favorite creatures" theme – a FEW favorite creatures from air, land, and water. Then we set to work making stencil designs to fit the squares. We tried and eliminated a butterfly, a bear, a frog, and a turtle. Our "keepers" were a bird, a puppy, a whale, a bunny, and an elephant.

Scattered across the quilt, the birds appear mainly on yellow squares, the puppies on green, the bunnies on pink, and the whales on blue. Some face east, others travel west, all in a playful but not always predictable fashion. A lone elephant found its special place. When I had completed the quilting, David took a creature inventory: 23 birds, 21 bunnies, 18 puppies, 7 whales, and 1 elephant. How many elephants do you need on one crib quilt, we wondered.

David is talking about his next quilt. A friend has given us a stack of colored kerchief scraps. I think I'll give David free rein to design his own project.

His interest in the Featherweight has not subsided. He loves to do the routine "oil and lube" job. Some mornings he comes to the kitchen, knowing I'll be quilting during the day, and asks, "Is it time for me to oil the machine again?"

Favorite Creatures was a delightful project for David and me. Step by step we conceived and created a quilt together. We both like to wonder about the children that will be snuggled beneath our cuddly creatures, about the grown-ups that will tuck them in.

I had not expected my son to show such enthusiasm for quilting. In our house, we have always observed "An Equal Opportunity Household" policy. Up until recently I thought it applied to cooking, cleaning, putting groceries away, and taking out the garbage. Now I know it also includes quilting.

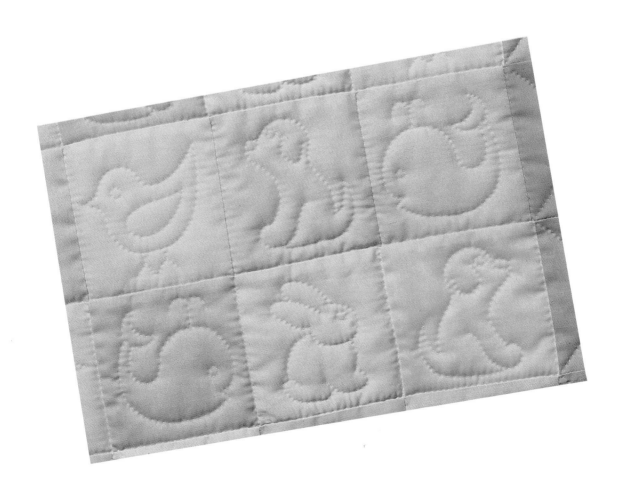

FAVORITE CREATURES CRIB QUILT

FOR STARTERS

The following list will help you enjoy a smooth start and steady progress in your work on the Favorite Creatures crib quilt. It contains a variety of general information about making the quilt:

- Wash and press all fabrics before you begin.
- A minimum of 4 fabrics can be used, but a larger variety of colors will enhance the design.
- A mixture of light and medium pastel fabrics in solid colors is needed.
- All seams are ¼".
- Only one template (a 4" square) is required.
- This pattern can be pieced very quickly by machine. It may also be pieced by hand. For machine-piecing, include the ¼" seam allowances on the template. For hand-piecing, make the template without seam allowances, and add them when marking and cutting the fabrics.
- Construction is by horizontal rows.
- The cream-colored borders are 3" wide.
- Five "creature" shapes are used for the decorative quilting.
- The finished size for the Favorite Creatures crib quilt is 42" x 54".

SUPPLIES

Use 44"/45" wide cotton or cotton/polyester blend fabrics.

Quilt Top:

Light pastel solids: A variety of scraps to total about 2½ yards, or ½ yard each of 5 fabrics: light blue, pink, yellow, light green, and lavender.

Medium pastel solids: A variety of scraps to total about 1¼ yards, or ⅜ yards each of 4 fabrics in medium shades of blue, green, lavender, and aqua.

Cream colored solid (for borders): 1½ yards

Binding: 1 yard of medium aqua solid

Backing: 1¾ yards of good quality unbleached muslin

Batting: Use a 45" x 60" (crib size) bonded polyester batt.

OTHER SUPPLIES

- Iron
- Material for templates
- Marking pencils or soap chips
- Scissors (for paper and fabric)
- Rulers
- Sewing machine
- Thread to match fabrics
- Pins
- Thread or safety pins for basting
- Quilting needles
- 1 spool of natural color quilting thread
- Thimble
- Long straightedge
- Hoop or frame for quilting

READY TO WORK

COLOR and FABRIC KEY
L= Light Solid
M= Medium Solid
C= Cream Color

TEMPLATE
Begin by making a sturdy plastic or cardboard template of the 4" square. For machine-piecing, add the ¼" seam allowance to all four sides of the template. Be sure to note the suggested grain line.

CUTTING

Begin with the Light Solid (L) fabrics. Cut a total of 70 squares from a variety of colors, OR, if you are using only 5 fabrics, cut 14 squares from each of the 5 fabrics.

Continue with the Medium Solid (M) fabric. Cut a total of 38 squares from a variety of colors, OR, if you are using only 4 fabrics, cut 10 squares from each on the 4 fabrics. (You will have 2 extra squares.) Cut the following borders from the Cream Color (C) fabric:

Cut 2 side borders 3½" x 48½" (seams included)

Cut 2 end borders 3½" x 42½" (seams included)

PUTTING IT TOGETHER

DESIGN

Now is the time to arrange your squares into a design of your choice. Using a suggested grid of 9 squares across and 12 squares down, place the pieces on a large flat surface (a bed or floor will do). Begin with the Light (L) squares. Make an arrangement of 7 squares across and 10 squares down. Add a row of Medium (M) squares all around. Rearrange squares until you have a suitable design. The quilt pictured

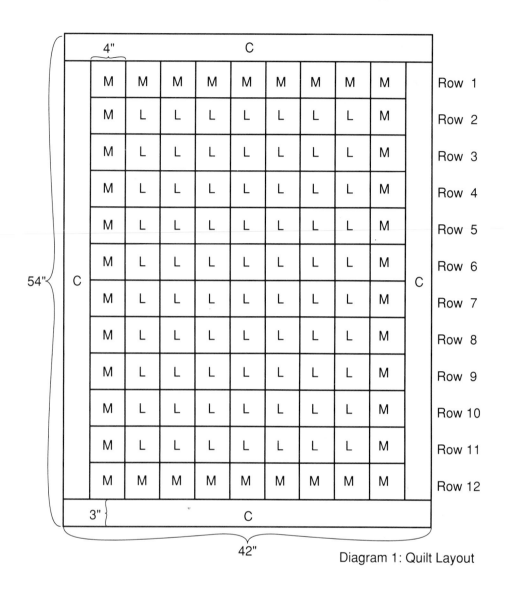

Diagram 1: Quilt Layout

Diagram 2: Row #1

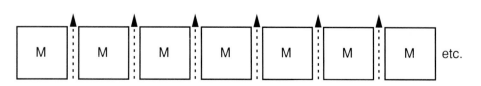

Diagram 3: Row #1 Piecing

here is set in a random fashion with all the light fabrics in the center, surrounded by the medium fabrics.

PIECING

Refer to Diagram 1 for the general layout of the pictured quilt. It is pieced in 12 horizontal rows, each consisting of 9 squares. Begin with Row 1, as shown in Diagram 2. It consists of only Medium (M) color squares. Stitch these together in short vertical seams as shown in Diagram 3. Press all the seams to one side, in the same direction.

Continue piecing Rows 2 through 12, using Diagram 1 as your guide. Note that Rows 2 through 11 have a Medium (M) color square at each end, with 7 Light (L) squares between them. Row 12 (like Row 1) is made up entirely of Medium (M) colors. Press the seams of Row 2 to one side, in the opposite direction of Row 1. Press all the even-numbered rows like Row 2 and all the odd-numbered rows like Row 1.

After all the rows are pieced and pressed, join them in the long horizontal seams, being careful to match and "butterfly" the seams at each junction. This should happen naturally if the rows have been pressed as suggested. Press all the horizontal seams to one side.

BORDERS

Add the 3" Cream color (C) borders. Attach the side borders first, then the ends. This completes the quilt top.

THE FINISHING TOUCH

QUILTING

Place the 1¾ yards of muslin backing fabric right side down on a large flat surface. Smooth the batting over it. Place the pressed quilt top over the batting, right side up. Pin or thread baste the three layers together for quilting.

Make templates of the five

"creature" shapes: Bird, Whale, Puppy, Bunny, and Elephant. Generally, mark birds on yellow fabrics, whales on blue, puppies on green, bunnies on pink, and elephants on lavender. (These suggestions vary from the pictured quilt.) Also, quilt "in-the-ditch" around each square.

Suggested quilting for the outer (Medium) squares and the border is shown in Diagram 4. This modified "cross-hatch" design cuts across both the border and outer squares, forming secondary shapes such as diamonds, triangles, and rectangles.

BINDING

Trim the batting to ½" larger than the quilt top, to allow for filler in the binding. Trim the backing to match the top. From the 1 yard of medium aqua binding fabric, make 3" wide continuous bias binding.

Fold the binding in half lengthwise, wrong sides together. Then attach it to the quilt front in a seam that penetrates all the layers. Turn the binding to the back and whipstitch it in place.

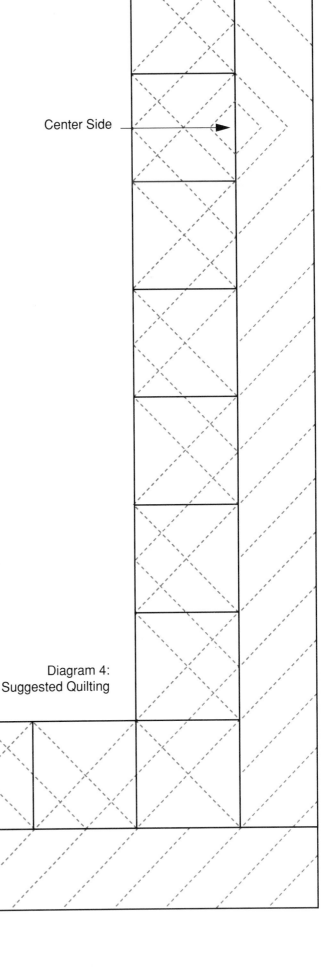

Center Side

Diagram 4:
Suggested Quilting

Center Bottom

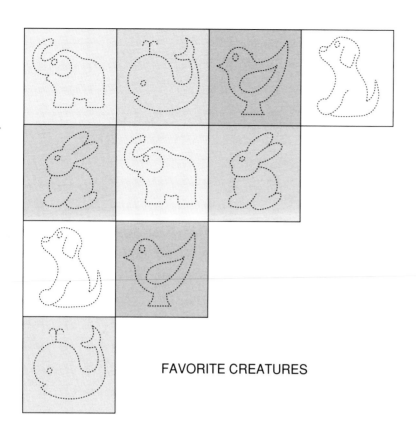

FAVORITE CREATURES

FAVORITE CREATURES

(Add ¼" Seams)

⟵―――――――⟶

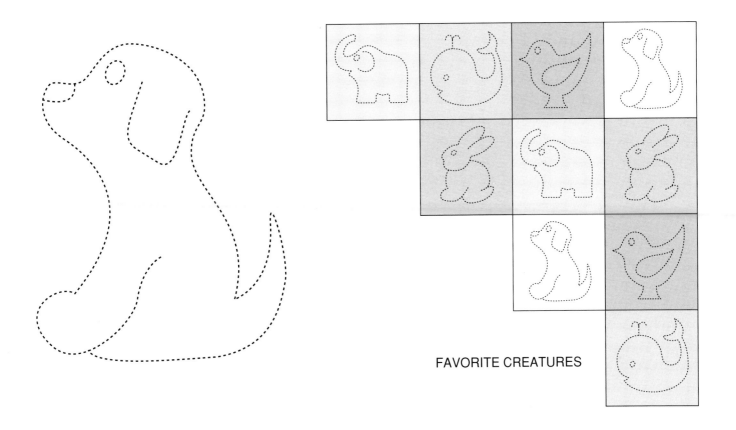

FAVORITE CREATURES

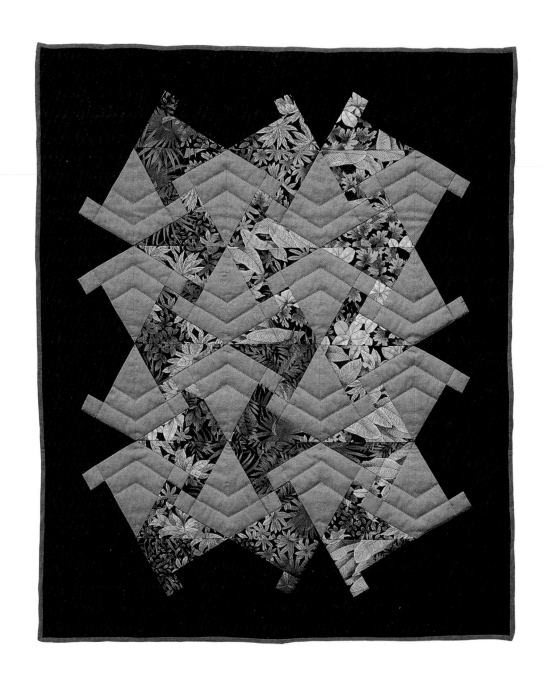

TESSELLATIONS AND OTHER POLYSYLLABLES
(ARABIC LATTICE)
QUILT BY PAULA JONES, EAU CLAIRE, WISCONSIN

TESSELLATIONS AND THE OTHER POLYSYLLABLES

"Tessellation" is one of those words heard among quiltmakers who have a propensity for geometric terminology. It is often heard in the same sentence with other polysyllabic words like "quadrilateral," "contiguous," "symmetry," "polygon," and "curvilinear." Tessellation is not some new quilt design phenomenon. Quiltmakers have been using tessellations since the day they first picked up two squares and pieced them together.

A tessellation is defined as "a careful juxtaposition (oops, another polysyllabic word) of elements into a coherent pattern." More simply put, it involves "same shaped figures that fit next to each other without any space left between," like the squares in a Trip Around the World or the hexagons in a Grandmother's Flower Garden. All triangles are tessellation shapes. So quiltmakers have been using tessellations for eons.

Creative tessellation patterns are featured in many of the drawings of M.C. Escher, the Dutch master who researched graphic techniques extensively. He experimented with rhythmic repetition and symmetric drawings, showing how a surface can be filled with similarly shaped figures which touch one another without leaving any open spaces. His published drawings and prints are a hallmark in the world of graphic arts. They have been an inspiration for contemporary quilt designs, as well.

The "Arabic Lattice" design is a tessellation pattern. Small squares and triangles with unusual angles come together to form an eight-sided shape that somewhat resembles a kite or an arrow. The squares and triangles are pieced into small blocks, which when set together, form the overall or tessellated pattern.

Arabic Lattice is an excellent choice for exploring and applying graphic techniques to fabric. That is why Paula Jones selected it for this wall quilt. Paula is a mathematician by profession, and there is plenty in her rendition of Arabic Lattice to confirm this, such as her precise piecing and her carefully placed quilting stitches. The rhythmic quality of her work is reflected in her choice of design and placement of fabrics.

Paula's quilt is proof that successful design can be achieved with just three fabrics. The lovely floral print captures the viewer's attention. The rosy solid enhances the floral fabric and the rich black intensifies the other colors. Her quilting lines are placed to complement the pattern shapes, piecing lines, and colors. The sum total is a quilt of simplicity and elegance.

Arabic Lattice is a good choice if you are looking for something out of the ordinary, something which offers a wee bit of a challenge. I would not call it a difficult pattern, but it will help to have your wits about you when you are piecing Arabic Lattice. All the steps are thoroughly explained and illustrated in detail to assist you.

ARABIC LATTICE

FOR STARTERS

The following list will help you enjoy a smooth start and steady progress in your work on the Arabic Lattice quilt. It contains a variety of general information about making the quilt:

- Wash and press all fabrics before you begin.
- Three fabrics are required: a light solid, a dark solid, and a bold print.
- All seams are ¼".
- For templates (patterns of the quilt pieces) use sturdy plastic, cardboard, or sandpaper, and be sure to note grain lines.
- Piecing may be done by hand or machine. For hand-piecing, make the templates without seam allowances, and add them when marking and cutting the fabrics. For machine-piecing, include the ¼" seam allowances on the templates.
- Only 3 templates are needed– a small square, a large square, and a triangle, which must be reversed when cutting some of the fabric
- Twenty-six (26) pieced blocks and four (4) plain blocks are needed.
- Each pieced block is 5½" square, finished.
- The finished size for the Arabic Lattic quilt is 27½" x 33".

SUPPLIES

Use 44"/45" wide cotton or cotton/ polyester blend fabrics.

Quilt Top:
  Light Solid (Coral): ½ yard
  Dark Solid (Black): 1 yard
  Bold Print (Coral/Black): ½ yard
Binding: ½ yard Medium Coral
Backing: 1 yard good quality muslin, OR an additional yard of the Light Solid above.

Black	A	B	A	Black	} Row 1
C	F	E	F	C↓	} Row 2
↓D	E	F	E	D	} Row 3
C	F	E	F	C↓	} Row 4
↓D	E	F	E	D	} Row 5
Black	B↓	A↓	B↓	Black	} Row 6

Diagram 1
Arrows Indicate Blocks to be Inverted

Batting: Use a piece of bonded polyester about 30" x 35", OR one-half of a 45" x 60" crib batting.

OTHER SUPPLIES
- Iron
- Material for templates
- Marking pencils or soap chips
- Scissors (for paper and fabric)
- Rulers
- Thread for piecing
- Pins
- Thread or safety pins for basting
- Quilting needles
- 1 spool coral color quilting thread
- Thimble
- Long straightedge
- Hoop or frame for quilting

READY TO WORK
COLOR and FABRIC KEY
L= Light Solid
B= Black
P= Print
R= Reverse templates

GUIDELINES
Although the Arabric Lattice quilt has few templates, the construction may be confusing, because several of the pieces must be cut with the template reversed. Half of the pieced blocks are mirror images of others. The easiest way to avoid

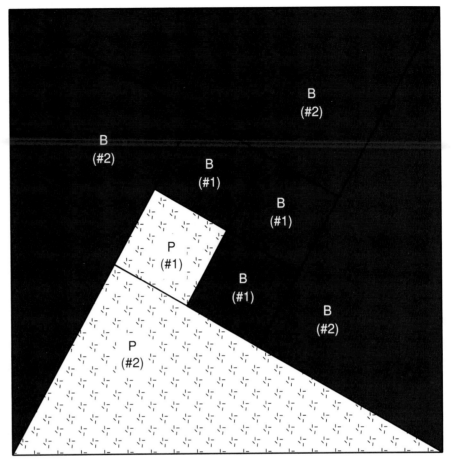

Diagram 2: Block A (Make 3)

errors is to think of the design as composed of several types of pieced blocks (designated A, B, C, D, E, and F), and arrange these blocks in six Rows as suggested in Diagram 1. The color photograph will also be helpful in clarifying the design and its construction.

TEMPLATES
Begin by making templates of the three Arabic lattice pattern pieces: small square (Template 1), triangle (Template 2), and large square (Template 3). Mark the grain lines on each template. Note that ¼" seams must be added on all sides of each piece. Also note that Template 2 (triangle) must be reversed for half of the pieces that you cut. These reverse pieces are designated with the letter "R" in the instructions and diagrams.

CUTTING
Begin with the Light Solid (L) fabric. Cut the following pieces:
Cut 32 small squares (Template 1)
Cut 32 (16R) triangles (Template 2)
Continue with the Black (B) fabric and cut the following pieces:
Cut 42 small squares (Template 1)
Cut 42 (21R) triangles (Template 2)
Cut 4 large squares (Template 3)
Next, cut the following pieces from the Print (P) fabric:
Cut 30 small squares (Template 1)
Cut 30 (15R) triangles (Template 2)

PUTTING IT TOGETHER
BLOCK PIECING
Refer to Diagram 2 for an illustration of one of the basic blocks (Block A). Collect the pieces

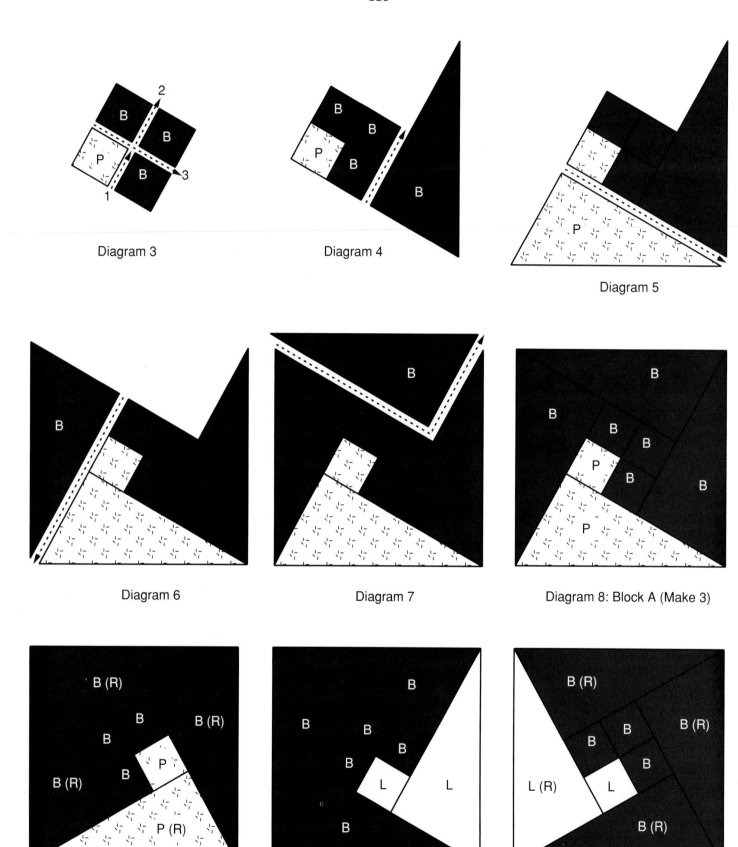

Diagram 3

Diagram 4

Diagram 5

Diagram 6

Diagram 7

Diagram 8: Block A (Make 3)

Diagram 9: Block B (Make 3)

Diagram 10: Block C (Make 4)

Diagram 11: Block D (Make 4)

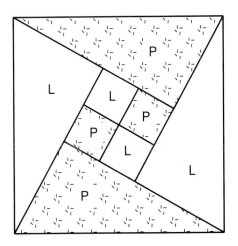

Diagram 12: Block E (Make 6)

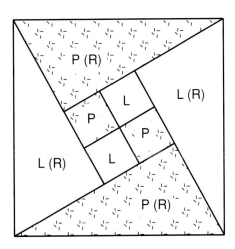

Diagram 13: Block F (Make 6)

necessary to complete this block– 4 small squares (3 black and 1 print) and 4 triangles (3 black and 1 print). Lay the pieces right sides up on a flat surface and arrange them into the block pattern. Then begin piecing in the following steps.

• First, join the 4 small squares together to form the center 4-patch unit, as in Diagram 3.

• Next, attach a black (B) triangle, as shown in Diagram 4. Stitch only to the end of the marked seam line on the small square.

• Continue by adding the bottom print (P) triangle, as shown in Diagram 5.

• Next, add a black (B) triangle, as shown in Diagram 6.

• To complete the block, add the last black (B) triangle on the top, as shown in Diagram 7. Pin this last piece carefully to match the seam line points. Stitch in a pivot seam.

• This completes Block A. Make 3 of Block A.

Continue with Block B, shown in Diagram 9. Collect the 8 pieces that comprise the block: 4 squares (3 black and 1 print) and 4 triangles (3 black R and 1 print R). Lay these right side up on a flat surface, to arrange the block. Then piece them

together, following steps similar to the ones for Block A above. Note that the joining of the triangle pieces will be in the opposite direction (counter-clockwise). Make 3 of Block B.

Refer to Diagrams 10, 11, 12, and 13 for the arrangements of Blocks C,D,E, and F. Make the number of blocks indicated on the Diagrams. You should have a total of 26 pieced blocks, as follows:

Block A-3   Block B-3   Block C-4
Block D-4   Block E-6   Block F-6

ASSEMBLY

Refer back to Diagram 1 and the color photograph for the layout of the blocks. It is probably best to lay out all 26 pieced blocks and the 4 plain corner blocks to be sure that everything has been pieced correctly and that the shapes will come together and form the correct designs. Arrows in Diagram 1 indicate which blocks must be inverted in order for the design to

come to completion.

Begin with Row 1, which consists of 3 pieced blocks (2 A and 1 B) and 2 solid black blocks. Join these in short vertical seams as illustrated in Diagram 14.

Continue by joining the 5 pieced blocks in Row 2, then the remaining Rows 3 through 6.

Last, stitch the six rows together in horizontal cross seams, to complete the quilt top.

THE FINISHING TOUCH

QUILTING

Place the quilt backing fabric right side down on a flat surface. Smooth the batting over it. Place the pressed quilt top over the batting, right side up. Pin or thread baste the three layers together for quilting.

With a straightedge and a washable marking pencil or soap chip, mark the quilting lines suggested in Diagram 15. Quilt with the coral color quilting thread.

BINDING

Trim the batting to ¼" larger than the quilt top, to allow for filler in the binding. Trim the backing to match the top. From the ½ yard of medium coral binding fabric, cut 1½" wide bias strips and piece these to a length to go around the quilt (about 4 yards).

Pin the binding to the quilt top, right sides together and raw edges flush. Stitch in a ¼" seam through all layers. Turn under ¼" on the remaining raw edge of the binding. Fold the binding to the back of the quilt and whipstitch it in place.

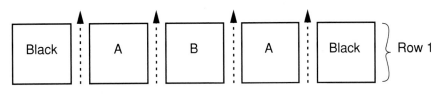

Diagram 14

Block E   Block F

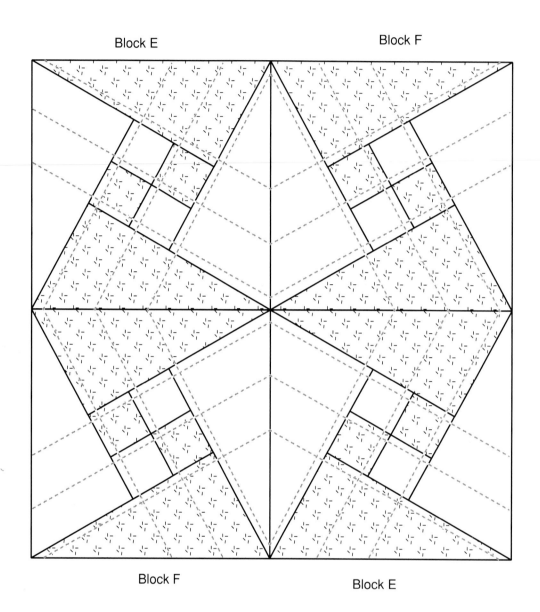

Block F   Block E

Diagram 15

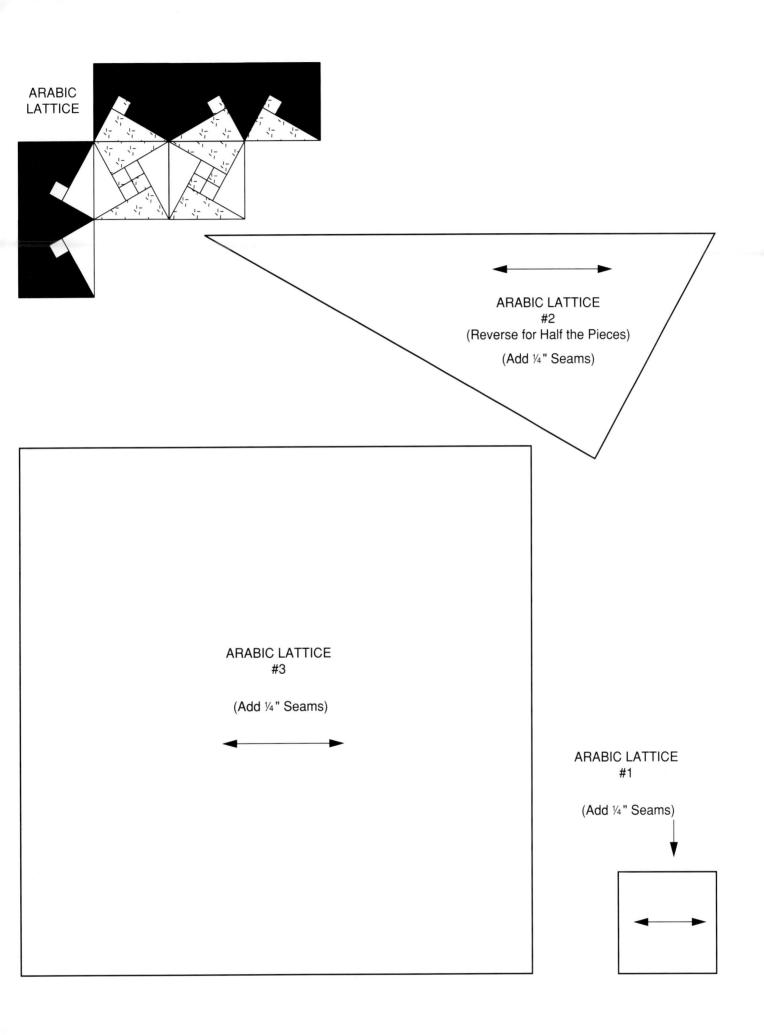

ARABIC
LATTICE

ARABIC LATTICE
#2
(Reverse for Half the Pieces)

(Add ¼" Seams)

ARABIC LATTICE
#3

(Add ¼" Seams)

ARABIC LATTICE
#1

(Add ¼" Seams)

CAPTURING THE HOLIDAY FEELING
(CHRISTMAS RIBBONS)
DESIGN AND QUILT BY PAT SIMONSEN, EAU CLAIRE, WISCONSIN

CAPTURING THE HOLIDAY FEELING

If you're searching for a project or gift idea to finish in time for upcoming holidays, Christmas Ribbons just may fit the bill. In addition to being modest in size (about 31" square), this medallion-style pattern is also easy to piece, whether by machine or hand.

Pat Simonsen has captured the festive spirit with a mixture of cheerful red and green holiday prints. Her colorful project is suitable for either a wall quilt or decorative piece for the center of a table.

Pat has used decorative hand quilting designs to complement the pieced ribbons: Clusters of green holly leaves and red holly berries on the snowy background and a wreath of holly in the center. Parallel quilting lines on the triangles help to highlight the motion of the ribbons.

Another design by Pat, "My Stars! A Computer Quilt," is featured elsewhere in this book – ample evidence that she excels in both piecing and applique design and technique.

Christmas Ribbons is not a demanding project in either skill or time. You, too, can break open your box of special prints and capture the holiday feeling.

CHRISTMAS RIBBONS

FOR STARTERS

The following list will help you enjoy a smooth start and steady progress in your work on the Christmas Ribbons quilt. It contains a variety of general information about making the quilt:

- Wash and press all fabrics before you begin.
- Four holiday prints (2 red and 2 green) and one white fabric are needed for the quilt top.
- All seams are ¼".
- For templates (patterns of the quilt pieces) use sturdy plastic, cardboard, or sandpaper, and be sure to note grain lines.
- Piecing may be done by hand or machine. For hand-piecing, make the templates without seam allowances, and add then when marking and cutting the fabrics. For machine-piecing, include the ¼" seam allowances on the templates.
- Christmas Ribbons is constructed with 4 large pieced blocks, 1 plain block, "filler" side triangle units, and plain corner triangles.
- Each large pieced block measures 11" x 11", finished.
- The decorative holly quilting designs are done in red and green quilting thread.
- Binding may be done in solid red or a pin dot.
- The finished size for Christmas Ribbons is 31" x 31".

SUPPLIES

Use 44"/45" wide cotton or cotton/polyester blend fabrics.

Quilt Top:

Red: ¼ yard each of 2 red holiday print fabrics

Green: ¼ yard each of 2 green holiday print fabrics

White: ¾ yard

Binding: ¾ yard red (solid or pin dot)

Backing: 1 yard of white

Batting: Use a 35" x 35" square of bonded polyester, or use part of a 45" x 60" (crib-size) batt.

OTHER SUPPLIES

- Iron
- Material for templates
- Marking pencils or soap chips
- Scissors (for paper and fabric)
- Rulers
- Thread for piecing

- Pins
- Thread or safety pins for basting
- Quilting needles
- 1 spool each of red and green quilting thread
- Thimble
- Long straightedge
- Hoop or frame for quilting

READY TO WORK

COLOR KEY

R 1= Red Print No. 1
R 2= Red Print No. 2
G 1= Green Print No. 1
G 2= Green Print No. 2
W= White

TEMPLATES

Make templates of the four Christmas Ribbons pattern pieces (#1, #2, #3, and #4). Mark the grain lines on each template. Note that the suggested grain line on Template #3 (medium triangle) varies when cutting the print fabrics and the white fabrics. Note that ¼" seams must be added to all sides of each piece.

CUTTING

Refer to Diagram 1 for the layout of the fabrics. Begin with the first Red Print fabric (R 1) and cut 8 medium triangles from Template 3.

Continue with the second Red Print (R 2) and cut the following pieces:
Cut 2 medium triangles (Template 3)
Cut 8 trapezoids (Template 2)

From the first Green Print fabric (G 1) cut 8 medium triangles from Template 3.

From the second Green Print (G 2) cut the following pieces:
Cut 2 medium triangles (Template 3)
Cut 8 trapezoids (Template 2)

Next, cut the following pieces from the White (W) fabric:

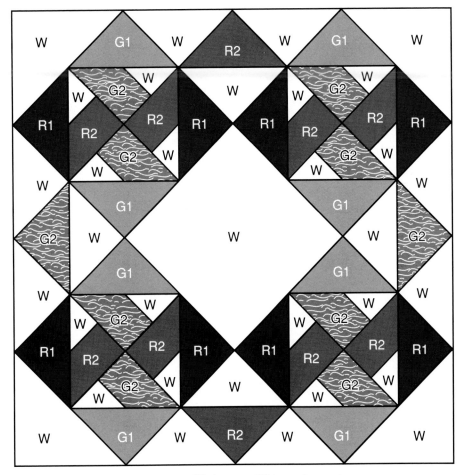

Diagram 1: Christmas Ribbons Layout

Cut 12 medium triangles (Template 3) with the grain line on the long side of the triangle
Cut 16 small triangles (Template 1)
Cut 4 large triangles (Template 4)
Cut 1 large square, 11" x 11" plus seam allowances, for the quilt center

BLOCK PIECING

Christmas Ribbons consists of 4 large pieced blocks and one plain white center square, as highlighted in Diagram 1. The pieced block is illustrated in Diagram 2. Collect the 12 pieces that comprise the block. Lay the pieces right side up on a flat surface and arrange them according to the diagram. Piece the block in

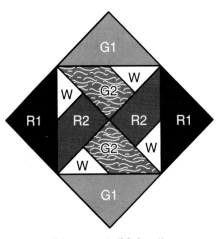

Diagram 2 (Make 4)

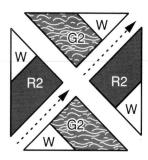

Diagram 3

Diagram 4

Diagram 5

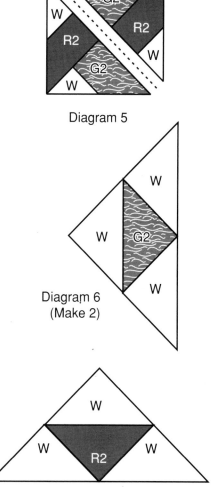

Diagram 6
(Make 2)

Diagram 7 (Make 2)

the following steps.

- Stitch a small white (W) triangle to a green trapezoid (G 2), as shown in Diagram 3. Make 2 of these. Make 2 similar units with the white and red (W and R 2) pieces.
- Stitch the units together to form larger triangular shapes, as in Diagram 4.
- Stitch these together to form a square, as in Diagram 5.
- Finally, add the medium triangles (G 1 and R 1) on each side of the block, referring back to Diagram 2.
- Make a total of 4 pieced blocks.

SIDE TRIANGLES

Refer to Diagram 6 for an illustration of a side triangle unit. Stitch the 4 pieces (3 W and one G 2) together. Make 2 triangle units like this.

Next, make 2 additional triangle units with three (W) pieces and one R 2, as shown in Diagram 7.

ASSEMBLY

Christmas Ribbons is assembled diagonally in three sections. Refer to Diagram 8 for the lower right corner section. Stitch the units together in the order indicated by the numbers, adding the White (W) corner triangle last.

Make a similar section for the upper left corner of the quilt.

Refer to Diagram 9 for the center section of the quilt. Stitch the two pieced blocks, the plain white center block, and the two white corner triangles together.

Join the three sections to complete the quilt top as shown in Diagram 1.

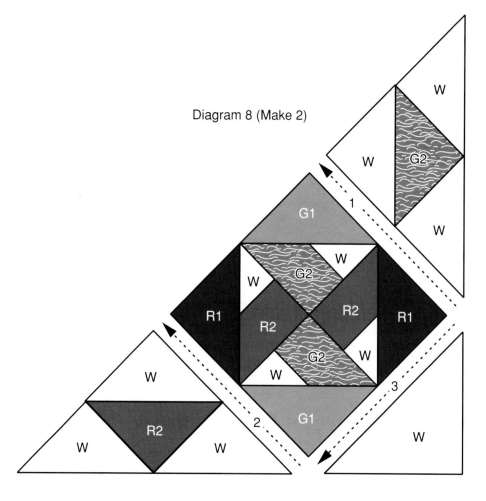

Diagram 8 (Make 2)

THE FINISHING TOUCH

QUILTING

Lay the 1 yard of white backing fabric right side down on a flat surface. Smooth the batting over it. Place the pressed quilt top over it, right side up. Pin or thread baste the three layers together for quilting.

Quilt "in-the-ditch" around the red and green fabrics and add parallel lines on the red and green pieces, as suggested in Diagram 10. Use red quilting thread on and around red fabrics and green thread on and around green fabrics.

Make templates of each of the three holly quilting designs (A, B, and C). Mark and quilt Design A in each medium white triangle (12 locations). Quilt Design B in the 4 white corner triangles. Quilt the holly wreath Design C (which must be doubled) in the center white square. Use green thread for the leaves and red thread for the berries.

BINDING

Trim the batting to ½" larger than the quilt top, to allow for filler in the binding. Trim the backing to match the top. From the ¾ yard of red binding fabric, make 3" wide continuous bias binding.

Fold the binding in half lengthwise, wrong sides together. Then attach it to the quilt front in a seam that penetrates all the layers. Turn the binding to the back and whipstitch it in place.

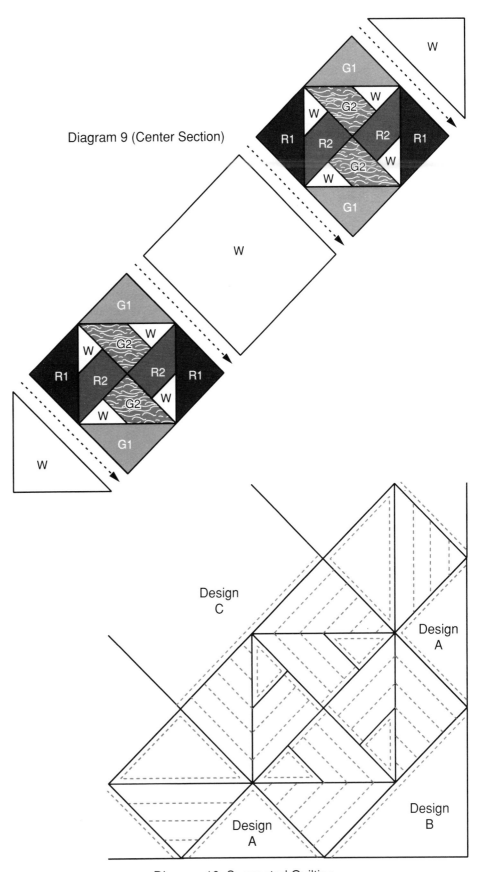

Diagram 9 (Center Section)

Diagram 10: Suggested Quilting

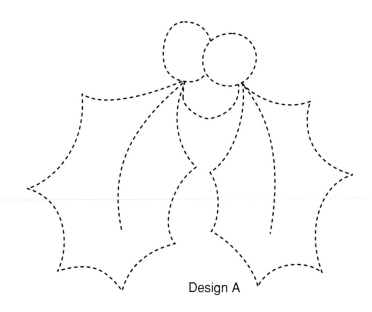

Design A

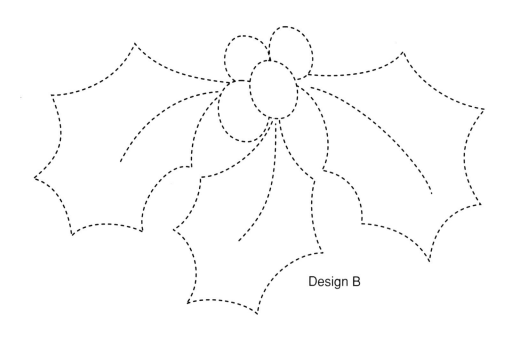

Design B

Design C (½ of Design)

CHRISTMAS RIBBONS

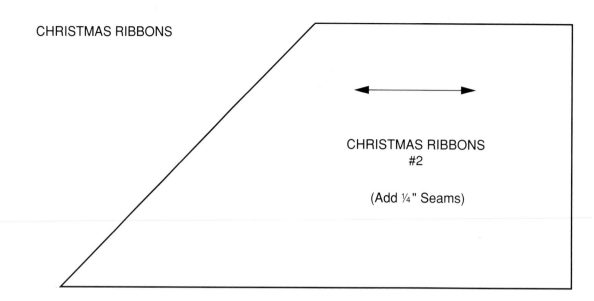

CHRISTMAS RIBBONS
#2

(Add ¼" Seams)

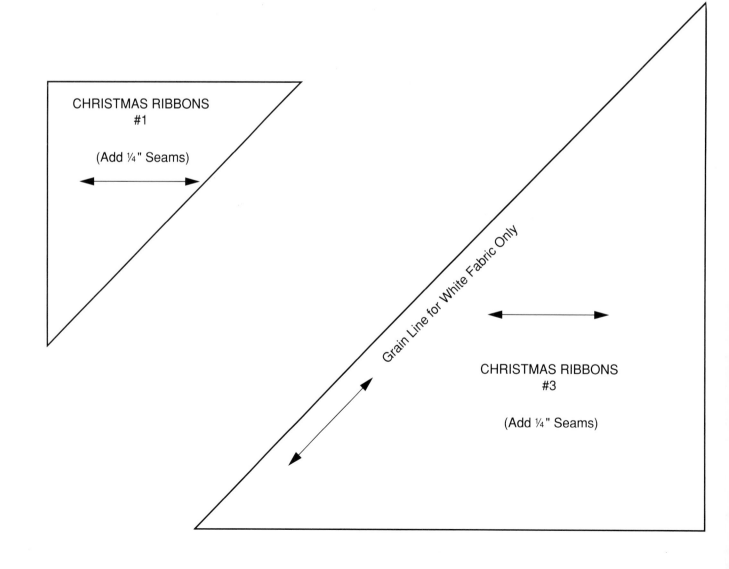

CHRISTMAS RIBBONS
#1

(Add ¼" Seams)

Grain Line for White Fabric Only

CHRISTMAS RIBBONS
#3

(Add ¼" Seams)

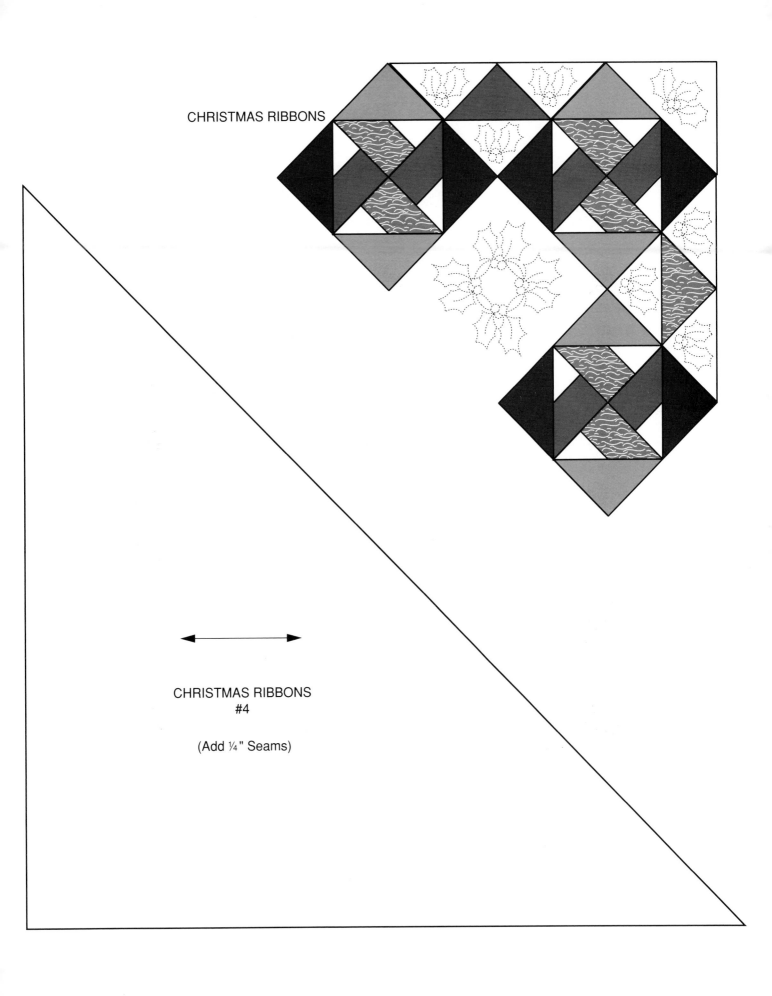

CHRISTMAS RIBBONS

CHRISTMAS RIBBONS
#4

(Add ¼" Seams)

SIX HUNDRED POUNDS OF EXTRA FANCY RICE
(RICE BAG QUILT)
QUILT BY THE AUTHOR

SIX HUNDRED POUNDS OF EXTRA FANCY RICE

The use of bags and sacks in quilts, wearables, and decorative objects is making a comeback. For many people, these items bring back memories from a time when thrifty homemakers recycled flour bags and sugar sacks into quilts and other household necessities.

Bags and sacks fall into that humble category of "other textiles" available to quiltmakers, especially quilters for whom purchased fabrics and cuttings from dressmaking were not readily available or affordable. Flour sacks, sugar sacks, tobacco bags, and salt bags were used extensively in the late nineteenth and early twentieth centuries. Sacks were often bleached, dyed to give colors, and pieced in simple patterns for quilt tops.

Printed feed sacks were an especially important source for quilters during the 1930s, 40s and 50s. In many rural areas, feed for farm animals was packed in cloth bags of a relatively loose weave, printed in various patterns. One feed sack was large enough for a child's dress; three would make an adult woman's. And four feed sacks opened into long rectangles and sewn together would make a quilt backing. Even the thread salvaged from opening and dismantling a feed sack might be used for quilting.

My grandmother used many kinds of sacks in her quiltmaking. I recently asked my mother if she had retained any of these sacks. A basement search revealed several kinds. Most, however, had been washed intensively and bleached to remove colors and printed information. Some were still faintly legible and will probably make their way into my quilt designs. The variety of my mother's and grandmother's bags included seed corn, flour, alfalfa seed, mink food, and sand and gravel.

My most recent quilt designs reflect my renewed interest in bags and sacks. Inspired by my family's collection of sacks and the availability of colorful cloth rice bags in our community, I recently completed a quilt featuring used rice bags. It included six muslin bags with colorful red and yellow emblems and Japanese, Chinese, and English lettering.

My second rice bag quilt, which is pictured here, includes two bag styles – a giant white crane against a red sun, and a large red rose and sword. I followed an ordinary design and construction process. First I opened the seams of the bags. Then I washed them to remove excess sizing and to soften the colors. Each 100-pound bag yielded a front panel about 18" x 33". Panels were pieced together and bordered in blue. The completed top was hand quilted with background clamshell quilting and highlighted designs on the bag emblems.

I have successfully used rice bags and flour sacks for bed quilts and wall quilts. I have also fashioned aprons, jumpers, and handbags.

The future of cloth bag and sack usage in quilts is uncertain. Some new authentic bags are still being manufactured, but many food and feed processors now opt for plastic or paper packaging, for sanitary and economical reasons. Replica and reproduction bags are available, but most seem to lack the nostalgia and charm of the real thing.

Given their availability, quilters and designers will probably continue to use bags and sacks. And while most quiltmakers in the past were reluctant to reveal the evidence of a feed sack or flour bag, today's quilters and designers will display them proudly in wearables and decorative items. During a recent lecture to a large quilt guild I wore a garment fashioned from a quilted rice bag, the design centered boldly across my bodice. I wore it shamelessly and quilters admired it. Later in the evening an elderly well-experienced quiltmaker said that years ago she, too, had worn bags, flour bags in her instance. She had worn them fashioned as her underclothing with the circular bag emblem strategically centered on her backside!

*For information about ordering new rice bags, send a LSASE to Quilt Enterprises, 6921 Timber Ridge Circle, Eau Claire, WI 54701.

RICE BAG QUILT

FOR STARTERS

The following list will help you enjoy a smooth start and steady progress in your work on the Rice Bag quilt. It contains a variety of general information about making the quilt:

- Information for ordering rice bags is available by sending a LSASE to Quilt Enterprises, 6921 Timber Ridge Circle, Eau Claire, WI 54701.
- Six large bags are needed for this quilt.
- Bags should be washed gently by hand to remove soil and excess dyes.
- Wash and press all other fabrics before you begin cutting.

- All seams are ¼".
- No templates are required.
- Two border fabrics, red and blue, are needed.
- The inner red border is 2" wide, the outer blue border is 3" wide, finished.
- The finished size for the Rice Bag quilt is 64" x 76".

SUPPLIES

Bags: You will need six large (100-pound) muslin bags. Address for a mail order source is listed above.

Fabric: Red: 2¼ yards (for borders)
Blue: 2½ yards (for borders)

Binding: 1 yard of dark blue

Backing: 5 yards of good quality unbleached muslin

Batting: 72" x 90" (twin-size) bonded polyester batt

OTHER SUPPLIES

- Iron
- Marking pencils and soap chips
- Scissors (for paper and fabric)
- Rulers
- Large 45/90 degree triangle
- Thread for piecing
- Pins
- Thread or safety pins for basting
- Quilting needles
- 2 spools natural color quilting thread
- Thimble
- Long straightedge
- Cardboard or plastic for quilt stencils
- Hoop or frame for quilting

READY TO WORK

BAG PANELS

Begin by opening the seams in each bag. Then wash gently in warm soapy water to remove sizing, soil, and excess dye. Press.

Lay each bag on a large flat

surface (a large cutting mat works well). Locate the center of the front panel on each bag. Use a large 45/90 degree triangle and a long straightedge to mark a panel 18½" wide and 33½" long on the bag front. (Seam allowances included.) Be sure the corners are square and the edges are parallel. Cut out each panel. You will need six panels for this quilt– 3 crane designs and 3 rose designs.

BORDERS

Cut the following pieces from the red fabric (allowances for seams and mitering included):

Cut 2 sides 2½" x 70½"

Cut 2 ends 2½" x 58½"

Cut the following pieces from the blue fabric (allowances for seams and mitering included):

Cut 2 sides 3½" x 76½"

Cut 2 ends 3½" x 64½"

ASSEMBLY

Refer to Diagram 1 for the general quilt layout. Begin assembly by piecing the three bags in the upper half of the quilt (2 cranes and 1 rose) in ¼" seams, as in Diagram 2. Then piece the three lower bags (2 roses, 1 crane) in the lower half. Stitch the 2 sections together in a cross seam.

Next, add the inner red (2") borders, mitering the corners. Add the outer blue (3") borders to complete the quilt top.

THE FINISHING TOUCH

QUILTING

From the 5 yards of muslin backing fabric, cut two 2½ yard lengths. Keep one intact (about 42"). From the other piece, cut two 15" widths. Join a 15" width to each side of the intact center panel. Press seams toward the outside.

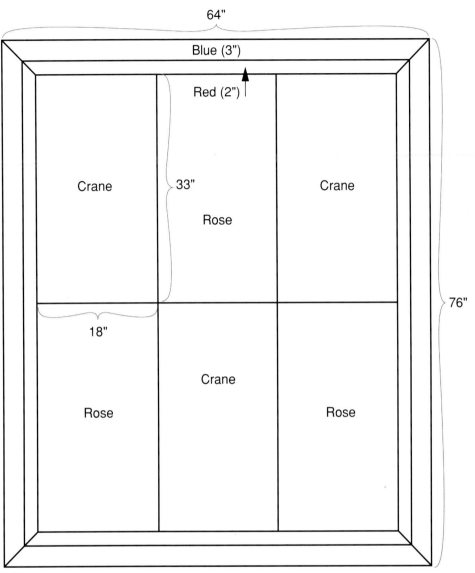

Diagram 1

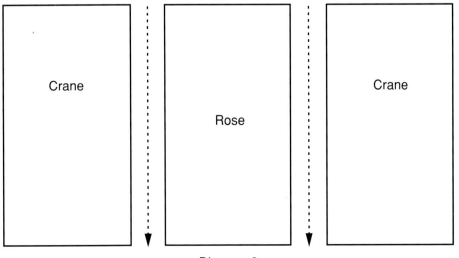

Diagram 2

Place the quilt backing right side down on a large flat surface. Smooth the batting over it. Place the pressed quilt top over the batting, right side up. Pin or thread baste the three layers together for quilting.

Make a cardboard or plastic stencil of the clamshell quilting design suggested in Diagram 3. Use a washable marking pencil to mark the clamshell pattern on the bags, as suggested in Diagram 4. Use repeats at 3" intervals in both directions. Use a long straightedge and pins to mark the 3" intervals along the bottom and sides of each bag panel. Quilt, using the natural color quilting thread.

Use a 45/90 degree triangle and a soap chip to mark the crosshatch quilting pattern suggested in Diagram 4. Quilt.

BINDING

Trim the batting to ½" larger than the quilt top, to allow for filler in the binding. Trim the backing to match the top. From the 1 yard of dark blue binding fabric, make 3" wide continuous bias binding.

Fold the binding in half lengthwise, wrong sides together. Then attach it to the quilt front in a seam that penetrates all the layers. Turn the binding to the back and whipstitch it in place.

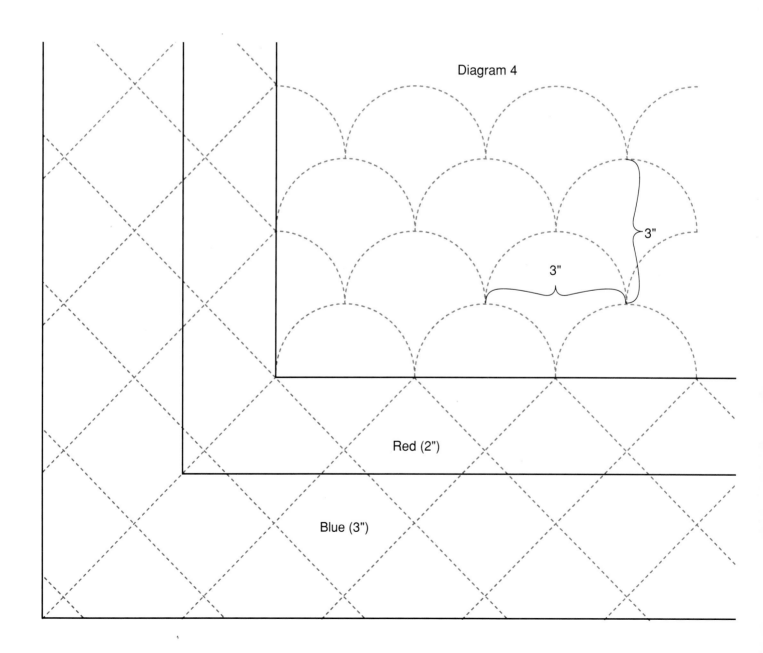

Diagram 4

Diagram 3

BIBLIOGRAPHY
Suggested References

For More Ideas and Information on...
Album and Friendship Quilts
Golden, Mary. THE FRIENDSHIP QUILT BOOK. Dublin, New Hampshire: Yankee Publishing, Inc., 1985.
Lipsett, Linda Otto. REMEMBER ME: WOMEN & THEIR FRIENDSHIP QUILTS. San Francisco: The Quilt Digest Press, 1985.

Attic Windows
Florence, Judy. AWARD-WINNING SCRAP QUILTS. Lombard, Illinois: Wallace-Homestead Book Company, 1987.
Leone, Diana. ATTIC WINDOWS, A CONTEMPORARY VIEW. Los Altos, California: Leone Publications, 1988.

Baskets
Boyink, Betty. BASKETS FOR QUILTERS. Grand Haven, Michigan: Betty Boyink Publishing Co., 1982.
Woodward, Thomas K., and Blanche Greenstein. TWENTIETH CENTURY QUILTS. New York: E. P. Dutton and Company, 1988.

Computer Design Quilts
Florence, Judy. AWARD-WINNING QUILTS, BOOK II. Lombard, Illinois: Wallace-Homestead Book Company, 1986.
QUILT ART ENGAGEMENT CALENDARS, 1985 and 1988. Paducah, Kentucky: American Quilter's Society.

Crib Quilts
Woodward, Thomas K. and Blanche Greenstein. CRIB QUILTS AND OTHER SMALL WONDERS. New York: E.P. Dutton and Company, 1981.
Pellman, Rachel and Kenneth. AMISH CRIB QUILTS. Intercourse, Pennsylvania: Good Books, 1985.

Lone Star
Boyink, Betty. STAR QUEST FOR QUILTERS. Grand Haven, Michigan: Betty Boyink Publishing Co., 1986.
LeBranche, Carol. A CONSTELLATION FOR QUILTERS. Pittstown, New Jersey: The Main Street Press, 1986.
Young, Blanche, and Helen Frost. THE LONE STAR QUILT HANDBOOK. Lafayette, California: C & T Publishing, 1988.

Ocean Waves
Fons, Marianne and Liz Porter. LET'S MAKE WAVES. Lafayette, California: C & T Publishing, 1989.
Martin, Nancy J., and Marsha McCloskey. OCEAN WAVES. Bothell, Washington: That Patchwork Place, Inc., 1989.

Rose of Sharon
Johnson, Mary Elizabeth. A GARDEN OF QUILTS. Birmingham, Alabama: Oxmoor House, Inc., 1984.
Marston, Gwen and Joe Cunningham. AMERICAN BEAUTIES: ROSE & TULIP QUILTS. Paducah, Kentucky: American Quilter's Society, 1988.

Sunbonnet Sue
Hinson, Dolores A., THE SUNBONNET FAMILY OF QUILT PATTERNS. New York: Arco Publishing, Inc., 1984.
Laury, Jean Ray. SUNBONNET SUE MAKES HER FIRST QUILT, SUNBONNET SUE GOES TO THE QUILT SHOW,
    and SUNBONNET SUE GETS IT ALL TOGETHER AT HOME. San Francisco: The Quilt Digest Press, 1987.

Tessellations and Illusions
Escher, M.C. THE GRAPHIC WORK OF M.C. ESCHER. New York: Ballantine Books, 1967.
Fisher, Laura. QUILTS OF ILLUSION. Pittstown, New Jersey: The Main Street Press, 1988.

Virginia Reel and other Fabric Mixtures
Beyer, Jinny. THE SCRAP LOOK (DESIGNS, FABRICS, COLORS, AND PIECING TECHNIQUES FOR CREATING MULTI-FABRIC QUILTS).
    McLean, Virginia: EPM Publications, Inc., 1985.
Horton, Roberta. CALICO AND BEYOND: THE USE OF PATTERNED FABRIC IN QUILTS. Lafayette, California: C & T Publishing, 1986.

Additional Beneficial Resources
Florence, Judy. AWARD-WINNING QUICK QUILTS. Lombard, Illinois: Wallace-Homestead Book Company, 1988.
Marston, Gwen, and Joe Cunningham. SETS & BORDERS. Paducah, Kentucky: American Quilter's Society, 1987.
Martin, Nancy J. PIECES OF THE PAST. Bothell, Washington: That Patchwork Place, Inc., 1986.
McClun, Diana, and Laura Nownes. QUILTS! QUILTS!! QUILTS!!! – THE COMPLETE GUIDE TO QUILTMAKING.
    San Francisco: The Quilt Digest Press, 1988.
McKim, Ruby. 101 PATCHWORK PATTERNS. New York: Dover Publications, Inc., 1962.
INFLUENCES: TRADITIONAL AND CONTEMPORARY QUILTS. Spencer Museum of Art catalogue. Wheatridge, Colorado: Leman Publications, Inc., 1983.
Roberson, Ruth Haislip (ed.). NORTH CAROLINA QUILTS. Chapel Hill, North Carolina: The University of North Carolina Press, 1988.
Seward, Linda. THE COMPLETE BOOK OF PATCHWORK, QUILTING, AND APPLIQUE. New York: Prentice Hall Press, 1987.

For your Mental Stimulation
Miles, Elaine, editor. GUIDING STARS, A SAMPLER OF QUILTERS' FAVORITE QUOTATIONS. San Pedro, California: R. & E. Miles, 1989.